Moving Backward Castes Forward

Vishal Mangalwadi

(This is the third, revised edition of the book
earlier published as *Why Are We Backward?*)

First Edition (*Why Are We Backward?*) 2013

Second Edition (*Why Are We Backward?*) *2014*

Third Edition (Moving Backward Castes Forward) 2024 ISBN: 979-8-9887831-2-1

© Vishal Mangalwadi

Published by:

Sought After Media

1077 N Willow Ave

Ste 105 PMB 1010 Clovis, CA 93611-4411

www.SoughtAfterMedia.com

Email: manager@SoughtAfterMedia.com

Distributed by:

www.Triaze.com

Email: triaze@ruahtech.com.au

Designed by Praneeth Franklin

Gratitude

I am grateful to Dr. Ashish Alexander and David Linden for encouraging me to publish this third, revised edition of the book originally published as *Why Are We Backward?*

Oyila Veer, Miras J. Daliya, Andrew Jerome and Kiran Ajit Kujur provided the practical support. Praneeth Franklin designed the new cover. Thank you friends.

Now we need help (a) to translate this book into Indian languages and (b) to start the Education Revolution, which will move the backward classes forward. This Revolution will utilize available technology to take the world's best education to the poorest students in India's remotest village and slum.

Other Books by Vishal Mangalwadi

1. *The World of Gurus* - Vikas Publishing House (Delhi, 1977)

2. *Truth and Social Reform* - Nivedit Good Books (New Delhi, 1985) and Hodder & Stoughton (London, UK, 1989)

3. *William Carey: A Tribute by an Indian Woman* (With Ruth Mangalwadi), Nivedit Good Books (New Delhi, 1992). Expanded edits of this book were subsequently published under various titles in the UK, S. Korea, China, USA, Mexico, Brazil, etc. The current edition in print is called, *The Father of Modern India: William Carey,* Sought After Media (Clovis, CA 2024).

4. *In Search of Self: Beyond the New Age* (Hodder & Stoughton London, 1991) and IVP (Downer's Grove, IL, 1992) published as *When The New Age Gets Old: Looking For a Greater Spirituality*

5. *What Liberates A Woman: The Story of Pandita Ramabai—A Builder of Modern India* (Main author - Nicol MacNicol, Introduction by Vishal Mangalwadi) - Nivedit Good Books, (New Delhi, 1996)

6. *Dear Rajan: Letters to a New Believer* GLS (Bombay, 1995)

7. *Missionary Conspiracy: Letters to a Postmodern Hindu* - Nivedit Good Books (Mussoorie, 1996)

8. *India: The Grand Experiment* - Pippa Rann Books, (UK 1997)

9. *Corruption vs. True Spirituality* (Incorporating *True Spirituality* by Francis Schaefer) - Nivedit Good Books (Mussoorie, 1998)

10. *Why Must You Convert?* - Nivedit Good Books, (Mussoorie, 1999)

11. *The Bible in India* (Wisdom from India Series) - Nivedit Good Books (Mussoorie, 2000)

12. *Astrology* (Wisdom from India Series) - Nivedit Good Books,

(Mussoorie, 2000)

13. *Fascism: Modern and Postmodern* (Main author - Gene Edward Veith) - Nivedit Good Books (Mussoorie, 2000)

14. *The Quest For Freedom & Dignity: Caste, Conversion & Cultural Revolution* - GLS Publishing, (Bombay, 2001)

15. *Spirituality of Hate: A Futuristic Perspective on Indo-Pakistan Conflict* - Horizon Printers & Publishers, (Delhi, 2002)

16. *Burnt Alive: The Stains and the God They Loved* (with Babu Verghese, Vijay Martis and others) - GLS Publishing, (Bombay, 2006)

17. *Truth and Transformation: A Manifesto for Ailing Nations* - YWAM Publishing, (Seattle, 2009)

18. *Obama, The Presidency and the Bible* (Pasadena, 2008)

19. *The Book That Made Your World: How the Bible Created the Soul of Western Civilization* - Thomas Nelson Inc. (Nashville, 2011)

20. *Why Are We Backward?: Roots, Myths and True Hope for Development* - Forward Press, (New Delhi, 2013). Now being published as *Moving Backward Castes Forward*.

21. *The Gospel and the Plough* (Main author - Sam Higginbottom) - Nivedit Good Books, (Mussoorie, 2016)

22. *This Book Changed Everything: The Bible's Amazing Impact on Our World* - Sought After Media (Pasadena, 2019)

23. *Don't Let Schooling Stand In The Way of Education* (Main author - Darrow L. Miller) - Credo House Publishers, 2021

24. *The Third Education Revolution: From Home School to Church College* (Editor and Co-author) - Sought After Media, (Pasadena, 2021)

25. *Conversion: The Revolution India Needs* - Sought After Media,

(Clovis, 2023)

26. *Healing the Open Wounds of Islam* (An abridged German edition has been published. The English language edition is in the pipeline)

27. *GIRL: Abort or Empower Her* (co-author, Ruth Mangalwadi) Sought After Media (Clovis, 2023)

Contents

Foreword

An Incisive Critique of Hindu Backwardness

KANCHA ILAIAH

(Former Head of Department, Political Science,
Osmania, University, Hyderabad)

Vishal Mangalwadi is a progressive Christian writer whose writings have influenced a lot of Christian and non-Christian people across the world. His new book *Why Are We Backward?* is, at its core, aimed at addressing the whole system of Indian education, including the hot-button issue of reservations. The book is a collection of articles published first in the *FORWARD* Press magazine. Most of these articles were meant to be a comment on a variety of topical issues, but as the writer himself says, the book as a whole, addresses a common theme of educational backwardness.

Mangalwadi sees both the advantages and disadvantages of the reservation system and, like Kanshi Ram, advocates social transformation in place of social engineering. He sees the present education system as a subset of the Hindu, caste-centred, inegalitarian system. Indian backwardness essentially is Hindu backwardness. The caste system is based on the Hindu god's (Brahma's) notion of fourfold varna, which is actually a satanic creation.

Israeli society in the pre-Jesus period was as badly divided as our own. Gentiles and Samaritans were like Shudras and Ati-shudras—unclean and untouchable. Pharisees, who considered themselves divinely favoured, did not associate with them in order to avoid getting polluted. But Jesus Christ's socio-spiritual revolution challenged that evil religious system. The Lord Jesus taught his disciples, such as Peter, to not call anyone "impure" or "unclean" because God does not practice favouritism (Acts 10:9-34).

The majority of tribes' people in Jesus's time were people from the toiling classes; Jesus himself was a carpenter (badhai). In contemporary Indian terms, Jesus would be an MBC, a member of the most backward class among the OBCs. His forefather David, who later became the greatest Jewish king, was a shepherd (gadariya).

The Samaritans were untouchable outcastes, more or less like Dalits. The few Gentiles (non Jews) in the society were mostly representatives of the imperial power, Rome, and were hated like, say, yavanas and malechhas in India, especially by the Pharisees.

Pharisees themselves were more or less like the Brahmins of India during the freedom struggle. They were against the Roman imperial rulers but were also against any spiritual and social equality. They did not want to interact with common tribespeople, Samaritans, and Gentiles. They treated Samaritans as untouchables, and they were hypocritical towards Gentiles. The backward sections in that society had limited spiritual, social, and political rights, which were under the tight control of the Pharisees and the Sadducees. Jesus rebelled against it and declared that God did not approve of it. This was the first major spiritual democratic revolution that gave the idea that God not only created all humans equal but gave equal rights to all people. This revolution was not allowed to reach India in a meaningful way.

In India, a much worse caste system continues to exist even today than what was seen in pre Jesus Israel. Many Indian Christians did not understand the anti-caste revolutionary struggle Jesus had launched in Israel, and they did not think of mapping that struggle on to the Indian anti-caste struggles that have been on since the days of Gautam Buddha. The Indian church (of all denominations) treated Jesus *mostly* as a salvator but not as a liberator who would empower them to find true liberation from caste oppression and exploitation.

Jesus was also a prophet of an educational revolution. Through his parables and teachings, he overturned a lot of popular notions of the time and challenged the hegemony of the Pharisees, who exercised tight control over knowledge. Most importantly, Jesus invested a lot of time in teaching his twelve disciples, who saw that he practiced what he preached. Jesus' example made it natural for the European Reformation to make education universal.

Unfortunately, by and large, the Indian church, though it carried out some social and educational service, did not invoke the ideology of Jesus to set aside the spiritual fascist ideology of Hindu Brahminism. It failed to understand the common spiritual and cultural ground between Pharisees and Brahmins. Unlike the Pharisees in Israel, the Brahmins in India have remained in spiritual power since the days of the Aryan invasions. They established a modern Hindu religion by keeping that spiritual fascism intact. And it continues even until now.

Mangalwadi in this book establishes that the Dalit Bahujan backwardness in India is rooted in Hindu caste backwardness. He also demonstrates that the West's advancement, including the advancement of science and technology, capitalism, and democracy, lies in the Bible's ethic and worldview. The earliest Indian to understand this progressive nature of Christianity was Mahatma Jotirao Phule. But his agenda was never carried to its logical end.

The church, particularly the Catholic Church, established good institutions of education—that too in English medium—with a view to mitigating Indian backwardness. But in reality, they ended up producing a very brutal, Brahminical, modern, English-educated class that treats even Jesus like a leper. English in the hands of upper castes and regional language education among Dalit Bahujan castes made the latter's backwardness even more pronounced.

Several experiments were carried out, and various attempts were made to uproot caste and backwardness. The post-Independence democratic state and the modern education coupled with the principle of reservation produced some organic intellectuals from among the Dalit Bahujan oppressed masses. But that did not, and does not, in any meaningful way abolish caste inequalities, primarily because those inequalities were sown by the Hindu spiritual fascist theory and practice of myth-making and caste observance, much before Jesus and Buddha were born. Though the Buddhist Sangha initiated a practice of spiritual democracy, Buddhism could not abolish caste in India as it was abolished in Israelite society after the Christian revolution. One factor behind this was that Buddhism did not believe that God commanded us to love even the untouchable Samaritans as ourselves.

Indian backwardness continues, without any hope of eradication, because the Indian masses remain stuck in Hindu spiritual fascism and primitive idol worship. Hindu spiritual fascism remains at the base of the Indian educational, governmental, social, political, administrative, business, and media institutions. It allows Brahminical forces to control the society and to continue that very backwardness that constructed the system of consent by which caste oppression and the socio-spiritual life of untouchability are preserved and modulated through the challenges, and in spite of the opportunities of modernisation.

In fact, it was Jesus, who taught the world that God understands all languages and speaks all languages. Thus English, and hundreds of other languages in the world, became the languages of prayer. Jesus also abolished worship of idols. In India, the Hindu gods understand only Sanskrit. The SC/ST/OBCs were not allowed to learn, read, and write that language. Thus, they were for centuries forced to be illiterate and superstitious, and now they are forced to remain outside the English language. India's backwardness is rooted in its spiritual backwardness. After all, the notion of political democracy emerged out of the spiritual democratic practice of the Protestant Christian churches.

The SC/ST/OBC masses of India need to move into any one of the spiritual democratic religions, and, unless they move away from idol worship, and revolutionise their spiritual selves, they cannot advance.

The process of revolutionising the spiritual self of the Indian masses is the only way out. Unless that is done, their educational backwardness cannot be eradicated. The post-capitalist world has proved with decisive evidence that education in one language (preferably English) that has an advanced script as well as a sufficient body of reading material, and an already-institutionalised scientific climate, is a must for any nation's development. In a country like India where caste and untouchability kept the productive masses illiterate for centuries as part of its spiritual fascist practice, spiritual democracy and modern English education are the only solutions. Unless they are deployed, the masses will not overcome their backwardness.

Most Indian churches have operated hand in glove with the spiritual fascist Brahminic upper castes of India for centuries, rather than aiding and abetting our liberation. Not that the church did not serve the poor. For almost two centuries, it has done some physical service to the SC/ST/OBCs, but the main empowerment of English education was sold only to the upper castes. In this situation, even the reservation principle cannot help the masses beyond a point. The majority of effort of the Christian service must move into giving English education to SC/ST/OBCs. And massive propaganda about Jesus' spiritual democratic revolution, as well as a campaign against idol worship, will do a lot. May this book hasten that process!

Preface to the First Edition

Vidyevina mati geli; mativina neeti geli; neetivina gati geli; gativina vitta gele: vittavina shudra khachale; itke anartha eka avidyene kele.

(Intellect vanished because of lack of education. Morals disappeared without intelligence. Progress died for lack of moral precepts. Wealth disappeared because of a lack of progress. The Shudras deteriorated, as there was no money. All these evil consequences resulted from lack of education)

— Mahatma Jotirao Phule, from *Akhand,* a selection of poems

"My final words of advice to you are: educate, agitate and organise."

— Dr. Bhimrao Ambedkar, speaking at the All-India Depressed Classes Conference (Nagpur, 18-19 July 1942)

Why are over one billion Indians "Backward"?

What can be done to help our Scheduled Tribes (STs), Scheduled Castes (SCs), and Other Backward Classes (OBCs) move forward?

Some "high caste" Hindus blame colonialism for backwardness. Mahatma Jotiba Phule (1827-1890) knew colonial rule firsthand. Having examined the role of the British in detail, he concluded that, in spite of all the horrible things that the British (like earlier rulers) had done in our country, it was Providence that used the British colonial era to begin our liberation from the slavery of the caste system that condemned us to social degradation, illiteracy, superstitions such as astrology, and grinding poverty.

Some of our intelligentsia thought (and perhaps still think) socialism can liberate us.

Others now believe that capitalism may be the answer. Mahatma Phule and Babasaheb Dr. Bhimrao Ambedkar saw education as the beginning of the solution. However, given our reverence for them, few of us pause to ask: What kind of education?

A brief look at the Russian experience may be instructive: The

Communist Party dethroned Russia's Tsars and captured power in 1917. Its leaders, such as Valdimir Lenin, shared the opinion that the lack of education was the main reason why Russia was backward compared to Western Europe and the United States of America. Russia's Orthodox Church had not invested spiritual energy in education, as had Protestant churches. Therefore, during the 1920s and 30s, Russia's communist government launched a massive campaign to eradicate illiteracy. It was called Likbez. Prior to that, only about 20 percent of rural children went to primary schools, and soon a majority of them dropped out of the education system altogether. Back then, "rural" meant most of Russia.

On 26 December 1919, Lenin declared, "Without literacy, there can be no politics, there can only be rumours, gossip, and prejudice." He went on to sign the Decree of the Soviet government, "On eradication of illiteracy among the population of RSFSR." This decree required all people from eight to fifty years old to become literate in their native language. The government set up 40,000 liquidation points to serve as centres of education.

Their commitment to education was so sincere that, even during the Russian Civil War (1917– 23), the Soviet Ministry of Education intensified its educational effort by assembling *Cheka Likbez*—the "Extraordinary Commission for the Liquidation of Illiteracy.

"The Communists did succeed in making Russia literate. Yet, Russia's communist government became one of the world's most corrupt, oppressive, and brutal. By the 1960s, it became clear that the Soviet economy was sinking—at least in comparison to that of the West.

The Soviet empire's political and economic bankruptcy forced even dedicated Communists to abandon their philosophy and open their minds to other ideas.

Meanwhile, however, the West's education was hijacked by non-spiritual ideologies. Education was separated from character formation and reduced to the impartation of information and skills. Western governments continue to invest heavily in education, but European and American economies too are stalled, if not already sinking.

Some cities in the world's sole superpower, the United States of America, the captain of the capitalistic world, cannot pay pensions to their retired teachers without borrowing from the rest of the world. The US government cannot repay the interest on its debts without borrowing more.

So, where will secularised capitalism end? Perceptive observers, who understand the factors that underlay the mindlessness of World War I, are recognizing that current capitalistic madness can only lead to another, more complicated, and costly war. Secularized capitalism that lacks intellectual means to distinguish ambition from greed may turn out to be worse than godless communism. If Western capitalism does crash, India will not escape unhurt.

In the 1940s, communism and socialism began seducing our intelligentsia, but capitalism began capturing our imagination after leftist ideologies collapsed in the 1980s.

In this book, I try to look beyond political and economic systems in order to explore the reasons for our backwardness. Although I conclude with an educational proposal to fight backwardness, the book goes deeper than "education" as popularly understood today. The book is an attempt to provoke us to come to terms with culture. In fact, the book examines some basic problems that are at the root of our plight.

The chapters in this book were first published as articles in New Delhi's first fully bilingual monthly *FORWARD* Press magazine. Often the topics were chosen to cover something that was happening that month. That explains the non-systematic treatment of the question, "Why are we backward?" as well as some overlaps and repetitions.

The publishers do not necessarily agree with every one of my assertions and conclusions, yet they gave me the freedom to express politically incorrect opinions and convictions. My views must have cost them readers at a time when winning and keeping every reader's loyalty was critically important to them. I think they stuck with me because they genuinely believe in fearless and robust discussion. Also, because from my father's side I came from a backward caste,

Kushwaha, and have devoted my life to identify with the poor, understand our backwardness, and fight it.

My personal history may explain a part of my passion—I do feel for my people, even though I did not grow up as one deprived. However, my passions could not possibly have turned into this book without friends who volunteered their time and energy to help me express myself. Most critical support came from Ivan and Silvia Kostka and Dr. Ashish Alexander, who edited and produced the book. Thank you, friends!

VISHAL MANGALWADI
California, September 11, 2012

Introduction

Moving Backward Castes Forward

Until recently, Bihar (including Jharkhand) was one of India's most resource-rich states. Yet, according to the 2023 state-census, over 84% of Bihar's population is "backward." That includes 36% Extremely Backward Classes (EBCs); 27.13% Other Backward Classes (OBCs); 19.7% Scheduled Castes (SCs); and, 1.7% Scheduled Tribes (STs). Jharkhand, carved out of Bihar, is poorer.

Who made them backward? How can they be moved forward? More importantly, is this unique to Bihar?

Nationwide statistics don't exist. Political parties and media, dominated by "upper"-caste Hindus, resist the call for a caste-wise census. For them, human inequality is a self-evident truth. The appropriate question is: Why is everyone unequal?

Many scientists assume that inequality is an inevitable consequence of Evolution, for some life-forms evolve more than others.

Indian sages taught that the Creator made some *varnas* (or castes) "low" or "backward."

Indian philosophers speculated that a soul incarnates as high or low, male or female, sick or healthy, rich or poor, because of its karma in previous lives.

If our sages and philosophers were right, then why did India's 1950 Constitution declare everyone "equal"?

Hindutva intellectuals say that the Constitution was crafted under the influence of a colonial (Christian) belief system. It was the Bible that taught that God created Adam and Eve (male and female) in His image. It teaches that all human beings are brothers and sisters because they have a common mother—Eve. The Bible's teaching on Sin also undermined inequality. 'All have sinned' means that a Brahmin priest is as far from the Holy God as a scavenger untouchable who is prohibited from entering holy temples. Most importantly, the Bible taught human equality by asserting that God so loved the sinners that He sent the Savior to reconcile rebellious sinners back to their Father. A King's child is a king, who manages his Father's kingdom of equal justice.

Indeed! Just five hundred years ago, European society was also divided into high and low classes. It was the Bible that challenged inequality, serfdom, and slavery. The battle for human equality began with the German reformer, Martin Luther. He was the first European to discover the New Testament's teaching that God adopts all sinners as His children so that they may serve their Father as priests and kings.

Bible translators such as William Carey—a cobbler by profession—brought the Bible's idea of equality to India. Along with his fellow missionaries, Carey began the mission to educate untouchables and girls. The invitation to become God's children appealed to the "low" or "untouchable" castes, for it made them "priests" (Brahmins) and "kings" (Kshatriyas).

The first Indian reformers who embraced the Bible's idea of human equality, without becoming Christians were Mahatma Jotiba Phule (1827–1890) and Sahuji Maharaj (1874–1922). Mahatma Phule realized that India's religious culture had forced poverty upon the masses by condemning them as polluted "low" caste or "backward" classes. Our people lacked socio-economic and religio-political power because India's religious system had condemned them to illiteracy.

In his 1881 book *The Whip of Farmers*, Phule wrote, "Without education, wisdom was lost, without wisdom, morals were lost, without morals, development was lost, without development, wealth was lost, without wealth, the Shudras were ruined, so much has happened through the lack of education."

Christian missionaries who educated Phule helped him understand that God had blessed the lower castes with minds as good as anyone else. Therefore, Phule believed that divine Providence brought the British rule to India to educate the "backward" castes. Imparting intellectual wealth to them would enable them to create material wealth and get out of poverty.

Therefore, along with his wife, Savitri, Jotiba Phule embraced the mission to educate the low caste.

Christian missionaries inspired Sahuji Maharaj to become a patron of "low"-caste students such as Bhimrao Ambedkar (1891–1956). Under that patronage, Ambedkar worked hard and earned the right to become the architect of independent India's Constitution. His education in the USA and the UK equipped him to give the backward classes the political right to equality. They could vote for politicians who best championed their causes.

Dr. Ambedkar knew that the constitutional right to vote and acquire political power was only a small beginning in the right direction. Social equality will come only when the right education changes India's soul. The truth of human equality can liberate the masses condemned to backwardness by false beliefs. That is why the Constitution gave citizens the right to education and conversion. Conversion is the freedom to repent from enslaving beliefs and embrace liberating truth.

Many people migrate from Bihar to Tamil Nadu because they find it better. In the 2022 survey, the State of the States named Tamil Nadu the best-performing big state in India, especially in terms of economy, infrastructure, agriculture, health, and education.

Tamil Nadu became a progressive state because of a grassroots Dravidian movement initiated by reformers such as E. V. Ramaswamy (1879–1973), known as Periyar. This Dravidian movement for self-respect challenged the Brahminical belief in Aryan supremacy. Although Periyar was an atheist, he built his movement upon the Bible's idea of human equality.

"Low"-caste reformers such as Phule, Sahuji, Ambedkar, and Periyar knew that the mission to uplift the downtrodden would not be easy. In contrast to them, Mahatma Gandhi (1869–1948) was born into the "upper" caste of merchants. He recommended Dr. Ambedkar to Pandit Nehru—India's first Prime Minister—because Gandhiji had embraced Christ's teaching that true spirituality involves the Uplift of All. Gandhi learned this by reading John Ruskin's book *Unto This Last.* He published its paraphrased version in Gujarati in 1908, calling it *Sarvodaya*. Based on Christ's teaching in Matthew 25:31–46, Mahatma Gandhi challenged his followers to serve the least and the last—the downtrodden.

Serving the oppressed and the crushed (Dalits) is costly because it requires us to "take up our cross." Militant Hindus assassinated Mahatma Gandhi for confronting India's false, unjust, and enslaving ideas. In this, Gandhiji followed the example of the Lord Jesus himself. The latter was recognized as the Christ, i.e., the Messiah or Liberator, because he defined his mission in the following words of God, spoken by the Jewish prophet Isaiah:

"Here is my servant whom I have chosen,

the one I love, in whom I delight;

I will put my Spirit on him,

and he will proclaim justice to the nations. . . . .

A bruised reed he will not break,

and a flickering flame he will not snuff out,

till he has brought justice through to victory.

In his name the nations will put their hope. (Matthew 12: 18–21)

The vast majority of Indians, including SCs and STs, are "backward" because they are "bruised reeds" or "flickering flames." Mahatma Gandhi, like other reformers, made his mistakes and compromises. Nevertheless, his moral influence upon the Congress leaders such as Pandit Nehru ensured that independent India pursued a policy of healing and strengthening the "bruised reeds"— the backward classes. Social Reformers, politicians, courts, the press, and rulers have done what they could. Now it is our responsibility to bring justice to victory in India's unjust social order.

A movement is needed to utilize available technology to make the best education available to the poorest child in the remotest village or slum. This education revolution must integrate knowledge and skills with truth and character building. It must impart wisdom to the masses.

This will require training shepherds to organize the poor into educational, medical, agro and dairy cooperatives. These cooperatives must be led by servant-leaders, not politicians. You are invited to learn more about this proposed movement by visiting:

www.ThirdEducationRevolution.com
Vishal Mangalwadi
September 17, 2024

PART I

THE ROOTS OF OUR BACKWARDNESS

Chapter One
A Brilliant Philosophy of Backwardness

"The agricultural school under Sam Higginbottom [in Allahabad] meets my ideal in vocational education."

—Mahatma Gandhi

On the 31st of December 2009, the glorious full moon of Paush Purnima began the Magh Mela in my home town Allahabad, now called Prayagraj (UP). By the time it ended on the Mahashivratri on 12 February 2010, as many as twenty million people may have taken a dip in the Sangam (confluence) of the Ganga, the Yamuna, and the mythical Saraswati rivers. What makes the Magh so magnetic for our masses?

The Sangam draws people to Allahabad because one drop of nectar spilled into it when the Aryan "gods" conned the dark-skinned native "demons." The gods had co-opted the demons into churning the ocean to get nectar. The fruit of their joint labour should have been divided equally. But our gods are cleverer than to allow for such fairness. They stole the whole lot and flew away faster than the native "demons" could chase them. Only four drops spilled along the way in Haridwar, Allahabad, Ujjain, and Nasik. Along with the godmen, now hundreds of millions of "backward" demons come to the Sangam every year to try to find the after-effects of one of those fallen drops. However, most return home poorer... complaining that they have been conned yet again.

During the last one or two thousand years, virtually every single Hindu philosopher, guru, godman, ruler, and merchant has come to Allahabad to the Magh or the Kumbh Mela, which is held once every twelve years. Many of these gurus claim to be gods. Some of them have raised vast sums of money abroad as well as in India to build great ashrams. But, during the preceding two thousand years or so up until I lived in Allahabad (1975), not one—not a single—of these gods ever built an institution of any significance in my hometown to move our people forward. Of course, the question of taking care of lepers never arose, even though they too come seeking favours from our gods and from the crowds that patronise them. Officially, leprosy has been eliminated in India, yet the UK Guardian newspaper reported on 24 March 2011 that 130,000 new cases are still reported each year.

Why don't our gods care?

Could it be that the philosophy our godmen promote is one of the root causes of our backwardness? I studied on the banks of the Jamuna, a few minutes' boat ride upstream from the Sangam, where missionaries from America built Ewing Christian College (ECC), Jamuna Inter College, and Jamuna Primary School to help turn Allahabad into a centre of modern education. Western missionaries, including educators, civil servants, judges, and soldiers, contributed to transforming a feudal Allahabad into a nursery of modern democracy. That is why my home town gave five of the first seven prime ministers to India: Pandit Jawaharlal Nehru, Lal Bahadur Shastri, Indira Gandhi, V. P. Singh, and Chandra Shekhar.

About a hundred years ago, the cruel indifference of our gods to the misery of our backward masses moved a professor with what is true godly compassion. His name was Sam Higginbottom, missionary professor of economics at ECC. He realised that teaching modern economics to upper-caste students was at best a very roundabout way of attacking poverty. At worst, it was giving sophisticated tools to forward-caste students to further exploit the ignorant backward castes. With a resolve to remove the misery of the backward communities, Higginbottom returned to America, studied scientific farming at Ohio State University, and raised $30,000 from churches there. He came back to Allahabad, bought the land across the river from ECC within sight of the Sangam, and established what became Asia's first agricultural college and an inspiration to Mahatma Gandhi himself. Higginbottom opened his school for all castes—especially those directly engaged in agriculture and related professions. He went beyond education to serve the multitude of despised leprosy patients who come to beg in our melas but do not find the nectar that heals. Higginbottom's compassionate leadership skills resulted also in the development of the famous Leprosy Asylum of Naini.

The Allahabad Agricultural Institute, now Sam Higginbottom University of Agriculture, Technology and Sciences (SHUATS), also organises an annual Agricultural Mela. I hesitate to confess the following because my postmodern critics will condemn me for disrespecting my heartless, oppressive, and mistaken culture. Yet the truth is that, even as a child, I was attracted more to the Agricultural Mela than to the Magh Mela. But it was only when I began to study Indian philosophy at the University of Allahabad that I understood the reason why our gods do not care for our backwardness.

The Samkhya Yoga stream of philosophy sees the material world (Prakruti) as evil. It is interested in isolating the soul (Purusa) from matter, not in improving our material lives. Vedantic philosophers go beyond Samkhya in declaring the material realm to be Maya—an illusory appearance. They accept the Buddha's First Noble Truth that life in this world is suffering. Therefore, they dedicate their lives to *escaping* life, not to improving it. The naked sadhus are the most honoured ones in our melas because they have (supposedly) renounced the world most completely. They love, value, and glorify poverty. So far from being able to remove it, they are not even interested in removing it. Sam Higginbottom was a professor who planted the intellectual and spiritual seeds of compassion that have flourished into India's agricultural and dairy revolutions, enabling us not merely to fight starvation and malnourishment but also to export food to other countries.

What made him so different from our religious leaders?

Higginbottom described his intellectual motivation, approach, and spirituality that drove his life in his book *The Gospel and the Plough*. His philosophy was shaped by the Bible, which teaches that the material world is neither evil nor maya. It is a real world that was created good. The Creator did not intend human life to be suffering. Suffering originally came (and continues to come) as a result of our own and humanity's sin. Our first parents, Adam and Eve, disobeyed God and brought a curse upon us and upon the productivity of this marvellous planet.

The Gospel, that is, the Good News, is that we do not have to go on costly pilgrimages to find forgiveness for our sin. Because of His grace, God has nailed the curse of sin upon the cross of Jesus Christ. The salvation that the Lord Jesus offers, frees us substantially from sin in our lives and enables us to fight the curse upon the earth. As God's truth, if we allow Jesus to become Lord of our lives, He delivers us from enslaving myths and the distorting power of our otherwise possibly misguided intellects. The Lord starts restoring God's creative image in us. He charges us to be responsible stewards of God's creation. As we begin to love our neighbours, He brings healing upon the land—agricultural as well as forest.

Sam Higginbottom began moving backward peasants forward because he followed the Lord Jesus, who said, "I have come that they may have life, and that they may have it more abundantly" (John 10:10).

Chapter Two
Religious Corruption and Backwardness

Our gods do not have to have a reason to be cross with us. It is their very nature to harass and oppress innocent citizens to extort appeasement from them.

An uncle of mine in Allahabad, who retired from the Indian Railways, once met a friend, also a retired engine driver. The gentleman lamented that his son was eligible for an appointment in his place, yet he did not get the job because he could not afford the hefty bribe that the department's officials were demanding. My uncle recalled the 1940s when the recruiting officers treated him with tea and biscuits and no one even hinted at a bribe.

Why has our culture and character degenerated into corruption? In his book *Slavery*, Mahatma Jotiba Phule explained how priests and pundits exploited hardworking Indians using the mumbo-jumbo of astrology. The courageous mahatma did not discuss political and bureaucratic corruption because, by his time, godly Englishmen had substantially cleaned up the once-corrupt British East India Company and, to a limited extent, India's own corrupt culture. Mahatma Phule's analysis can help us understand an important cultural cause of our degeneration. The late Mr. N. T. Rama Rao was a film actor who played the part of mythical gods in Telugu films. His popularity catapulted him into the chief ministership of Andhra Pradesh, and he, more than any other politician, brought astrology back into the public life of India. Mr. Rama Rao alienated his senior colleagues when he began to govern not as a team leader but as a god. Once, when he had to go out of India for a medical need, the Congress party tempted his estranged followers to rebel against him. That caused a split in his party, and he lost his position and power.

The people voted him back into power a second time. I was the national convenor of the Peasant Commission of the Janata Party. One day some members of Parliament from Andhra Pradesh came to our office at 7 Jantar Mantar Road, New Delhi. They reported that soon after becoming chief minister, Mr. Rama Rao summoned the legislators of his party, washed his feet in a basin of water, and made them drink it as an oath of loyalty to him. If the story is true, they took the oath but couldn't keep it for long. The party split again.

One fine morning, after Mr. Rama Rao became the chief minister for the third time, he stopped going to office because his astrologers and vastu shastries told him that the previous calamities had occurred because the entrance to the chief minister's office faced a direction where the stars were inauspicious for him. The national press reported that nine residential houses had to be demolished and a new road and gate built before he would go to his office. Within a few months of these new arrangements, his son and the computer-savvy son-in-law, Mr. Chandrababu Naidu, led a mediaeval-style revolt against him. They successfully ousted him from office. The poor man died of a heart attack.

Mr. Rama Rao's spiritual guides-cum-astrologers explained that this calamity overtook him because there are ten planets; the astrologers know of nine and had taken care to appease each of them. "Even the best of us does not know the tenth planet," they said, and "this tragedy is the influence of the tenth planet." Sometime after this event, I was speaking at a public meeting in Hyderabad. I said, "The politically powerful spiritual preceptors of this city may be correct; Mr. Rama Rao's misfortune may have been caused by the gods that had favoured the ambitious rebels. My question is: Why should our gods be inauspicious to Mr. Rama Rao? Wasn't he doing good for his people? He was selling rice for Rs. 2 per kilo to the poor. He had banned alcohol. He had promised saris to poor girls when they married. Downtrodden people loved him and voted for him. Why then should the gods be inauspicious to him?

The answer, of course, is that our gods do not have to have a reason to be cross with us. It is their nature to harass and oppress innocent devotees to extort appeasement from them. One day it's Saturn who is inauspicious to you; the next day it is Venus. One week it is Mars, another month it is Ganeshji that extorts appeasement. It was the late Nirad Chaudhuri's *Autobiography* (1951) that first explained to me the point that Mahatma Phule had made a hundred years before him— that the Indian character is corrupt because our gods are venal (easily bribed and corrupted). Nirad Babu wrote,

> But the most serious handicap from which Hindu ethics suffers is to be found in the universal and ineradicable assumption that the gods are venal The Hindu pantheon is as corrupt as the Indian administration... [because] the gods stooped to venality, the atmosphere in the temple naturally approached that operating in an Indian police station or the black market, and morality received its worst blow from what is popularly believed to be its patron and protector [i.e., religion). (Nirad C. Chaudhuri, *The Autobiography of an Unknown Indian*, Bombay: Jaico, 1964 edn), pp. 458–468.)

Why didn't my uncle have to pay a bribe in the 1940s to get a job with the Indian Railways? It was because that was the only period in our entire history when a particular religious ethos had checked corruption successfully; Mahatma Phule and Nirad Chaudhuri were not the only ones who testified to the fact that the eighteenth-century corruption of the British administration had been substantially cleaned up during the nineteenth century. It is, of course, right to hate British rule in India. Yet, the difficulty is that those who want to learn how to fight corruption in India have no successful model other than the success of British evangelicals, who cleaned up not only Britain but also British colonies.

It was Charles Grant who began the battle in 1790 to end corruption and reform the government of the East India Company. He came to Bengal as a private servant to a British civil servant but grew up to become a Member of Parliament and a director of the

East India Company.

The tragic deaths of two of his daughters started him on a spiritual quest. First his wife, and then he acknowledged that they were sinners. They prayed to Jesus for salvation from their sin. Prayerful study of the Bible transformed Grant's world-and-life view. When he returned to England, he joined a group of evangelical politicians, bankers, and philanthropists near London, known as the "Clapham Group." Along with the group's leaders, William Wilberforce and Zachary Macaulay, Grant began the battle to bring the company under the ethical demands of the Bible. That battle climaxed between 1833 and 1853 when his son Charles Grant Jr. and his friend Zachary's son (Lord Macaulay) enacted a number of reforms, including the new principle that civil servants would be recruited on the basis of merit rather than connections or bribery. A satisfactory account of that great story that created modern India is yet to be written, but what we already know is this:

The British Evangelicals succeeded in reforming the then corrupt Indian government because they followed the Bible's God, who used His power in human history not to oppress and extort but to serve, to wash the feet of His disciples, and to give His own life on the cross of Calvary to deliver us from the power of sin.

William Carey—Grant's younger contemporary, who became the Father of modern India—took the battle for India's regeneration deeper than Charles Grant. He wanted to reform not just the state but also our people. He worked on the dictum that a people could not be better than their gods. Carey mentored Indian reformers such as Raja Ram Mohan Roy, who learned from him that India could not be reformed unless it was delivered from her corrupt gods. Grant, Carey, and Roy were followed by reformers from Keshab Chandra Sen to Mahatma Jotiba Phule and Dr. Bhimrao Ambedkar who attempted to break the cultural chains of our slavery. We are still backward because their mission of delivering us from our corrupt gods remains unfinished.

Chapter Three
What Helped Holland's Gopals Press Forward?

Poverty, corruption, and a hellish society are only the initial fruits of sin.

Six months after our marriage, my wife and I went to live outside a village in Chhatarpur (MP) to do whatever we could to help our neighbours get out of chronic poverty. Some people heard about our work and invited me to England to speak at a conference on Simple Lifestyle and Economic Development. The plane from Delhi to London took off at about two in the morning. I was sleepy, but when Mr. Singh, who was sitting next to me, found out that I was living in a mud house, earning Rs 600 per month, he concluded that, more than sleep, I needed counselling. He made it his mission to persuade me to change my vocation, relocate to England, and become a businessman. He went on and on, describing how easy it was to establish a successful business in England. By 3.30 in the morning, it was getting difficult to pretend I was listening, but just when I was ready to tell him I needed to sleep, something intrigued me: While my English was poor, his was worse. I began to wonder how an Indian who couldn't speak one sentence of correct English could succeed as a businessman in England.

So, I asked him, "Mr Singh, why is it so easy to do business in England?"

He replied without pausing, "Because everyone trusts you over there."

I wasn't a businessman, so I didn't understand what trust had to do with the economic success of an individual or a nation. Had Mr. Singh defended capitalism, socialism, or communism, I might have become interested in listening, but his answer didn't square with any of the economic pundits with whose works I was acquainted. So, I pushed my seat back and fell asleep.

A few months later, my wife and I were invited to Holland to speak at the annual conference of one of Holland's largest charities that donates much money to NGOs in India. One afternoon our host, Dr. Jan van Barneveld, said to me, "Come, let's go get some milk. The two of us walked to the dairy farm through the beautiful Dutch countryside with gorgeous moss-covered trees. I had never seen such a dairy! It had a hundred cows, there were no workers on site, and it seemed amazingly clean and orderly. On our farm in Chhatarpur, we too had a small dairy of our own. Our dairy had two workers, but it was always filthy and smelly.

The contrast captured my attention because in our villages at least 75 percent of the women spent an hour or two every day collecting cow dung with their bare hands. They carried it in baskets on their heads to their backyards and patted it into cow-dung cakes for cooking fuel. Most families cooked the food in the same room where they slept. The poisonous fumes burned their lungs so that by the time the women turned fifty, they looked as old as European women who were ninety years old. The Dutch dairy surprised me because no one was there to milk the cows. I had never heard of machines milking cows and pumping the milk into a huge tank. We walked into the milk room, and no one was there to sell the milk. I expected Jan to ring a bell, but instead he just opened the tap, put his jug under it, and filled it up. Then he reached up to a windowsill, took down a bowl full of cash, took out his wallet, put twenty guilders into the bowl, took some change, put the change in his pocket, put the bowl back, picked up his jug, and started walking. I was stunned.

"Man," I said to him, "if you were an Indian, you would take the milk and the money." Jan laughed.

A few years ago, I told this story in Indonesia, and an Egyptian gentleman laughed the loudest. As all eyes turned to him, he explained, "We are cleverer than Indians. We would take the milk, the money, *and* the cows."

Back in Holland, in that moment of laughter, I understood what Mr. Singh had been trying to explain to me on the plane to London. If I walked away with the milk and the money, the dairy owner would have to hire a salesman. Who would pay for him? I, the consumer!

However, if the consumers are dishonest, why should the supplier be honest? He would add water to the milk to increase the volume. Being an activist, I would protest that the milk was adulterated; therefore, the government must appoint milk inspectors. But who would pay for the inspectors? I, the taxpayer!

If the consumer and the suppliers are dishonest, why would the inspectors be honest? They would extract bribes from the suppliers. If they didn't get the bribes, they would use one law or another to make sure that the sale is delayed enough to make the non-refrigerated milk curdle. Who would pay for the bribes? Initially the supplier, but eventually you and I, the consumers.

By the time I had paid for the milk, the salesman, the water, the inspector, and the bribe, I wouldn't have enough money to buy chocolate syrup to add to the milk. Without the flavour, my children don't like milk. Consequently, they are not as strong as European children.

Having paid for all of these things, chances are I would not have surplus money to take my children for an ice cream treat on Saturday night. The person who makes and sells ice cream adds value to the milk, whereas the salesman, the water, the inspectors, and the bribe add nothing. In paying for them, I simply pay for my sin—that is, my propensity to covet and steal. my neighbour's milk and money. The high price of sin makes it difficult for me to buy ice cream; that is to say, the price of sin prevents me from patronising genuine economic activity. My culture of distrust and dishonesty robs me of money that could be used to provide a better life for my children and productive employment for my neighbours.

My visit to the dairy farm helped me understand why a small country like Holland is able to donate money to a much larger nation such as India. It also helped me finally understand what Mr.

Singh, my fellow passenger, a semi-literate businessman, was explaining to me. He could say what political leaders and economic experts avoid discussing: that moral integrity is a huge factor behind the unique socio-economic and socio-political success of the West. For example, America is the richest country in the world with an annual GDP of around $14 trillion in 2010, but it allegedly had only $15 billion in "black money" in secret accounts in tax havens. By contrast, ours is a relatively poor country with a GDP of less than $2 trillion in 2010, yet wealthy Indians were reported to have hidden away $1500 billion (in 2010) in tax-evaded dollars in secret accounts in foreign banks.

Of course, the West's moral standards are now declining, and soon they may become as corrupt as us. But what made the West morally superior and, therefore, economically forward? The main difference is that while we in India were taught that we are God and that it is sport (game or lila) for Gopal (lit. cattle rearer) to steal (not only milk but also) butter and the milkmaids' (gopis) clothing, Holland was built on the Bible's teaching that we are sinners and that sin is not lila. It is a serious matter since it is a rebellion against God's Law: "You shall not steal." Poverty, corruption, and a hellish society are only the initial fruits of sin, including covetousness and theft. The ultimate consequence of sin is eternal hell for our souls. During the previous centuries, the people of Holland responded to the Bible's call to repent from sin, accept God's offer of salvation, and seek God's Spirit, who gives spiritual new birth, resulting in a morally transformed life. A life lived in the power of God's Spirit results in our moral transformation. It provides the energy needed to clean up corruption in society. Eventually it blossoms into an eternal line beyond the grave. It was this "Good News" of God's offer of salvation from sin and the Kingdom of God that became the cultural foundation of the modern West, the force that produced moral integrity, economic prosperity, and political freedom.

PART II
CULTURAL MANIFESTATIONS

Chapter Four
Temples or Dams?

We are created to govern nature—not to worship it. The river is not God.

In 1977, a group of young people invited me to their village in Chhatarpur. A minor flood had washed away their homes, crops, and cattle. So, they wanted me to start some relief projects for them. When I got there, my hosts showed me the pride of their village—a temple in the middle of the river. They said it was built a thousand years ago, around the same time as the Khajuraho temples.

I asked them, "Why do you think you are so poor?"

"We work hard," they replied mournfully, "for ten, twenty, or thirty years; we save some money, buy some animals, and build houses, but then a flood comes and washes away everything, and we are reduced to zero."

"A thousand years ago," I reminded them, "our forefathers had the ability to build such a grand temple in the middle of this river. It has withstood hundreds of floods. Did they have the ability back then to build houses on the banks of the river that could withstand floods?"

"Of course they did!" asserted my friends, pointing to the chief's stone house, up on the highest point in the middle of the village. "That was built around the same time as this temple." "Why didn't they then build strong houses for themselves?" I asked my friends, but without waiting for their answer, I went on to ask another question:

"A thousand years ago, our ancestors had the ability to build a temple in the middle of a river. It tells us of their engineering skills, their human organisation, and the surplus time and money they possessed. Do you think back then they had the ability to build a dam and canal system? Could they have said to the river, "We love you and we will make a home for you; please stay with us during the summer months and flow through our fields, but for the rainy season we will make a different path for you through the jungles, so you don't have to go through our homes?""

"Of course!" said my friends, "our ancestors were as capable as anyone else in the world."

"So, why did they make a temple instead of a dam? If they had made a dam, we would be richer than Switzerland, because in this climate, we can grow four crops a year. The Swiss have to work hard for only two crops a year."

My friends wondered where I was going, so I gave them a hint: "Did they make a temple because our ancestors feared the river and worshipped her?"

"Yes, of course, the river is our mother. It gives us life; when it is angry, it brings death and destruction. If it wasn't for the river, our village wouldn't even exist. Therefore, we revere and worship the river as our goddess."

My friends, as you can tell, were very devout. They worshipped many gods, goddesses, and even demons, but they also lived with chronic poverty. Over a period of time, I helped them consider if our poverty could be related to our superstitious beliefs and cultural values. I told my friends how about 3,500 years ago the great prophet Moses transformed a large group of Hebrew slaves, who came out of Egypt, into a mighty and prosperous nation we today know as Israel and the prosperous Jewish people around the world.

The most important factor that turned a backward people into one of the world's most forward communities was the Ten Commandments. The story of the giving of the Ten Commandments has been made into a famous Hollywood film. Mahatma Phule never saw that film, but he read the Ten Commandments in the second book of the Bible called Exodus. It helped him understand the most important secret of transforming a backward community into a forward people: They have to be liberated from superstitions that enslave them. A reformer has to make people lovers of truth. Therefore, Phule understood the importance of the first two commandments were the one Creator God, says:

> I am the Lord your God, who brought you out of Egypt, out of the land of slavery. You shall have no other gods besides Me.

> You shall not make for yourself an idol in the form of anything in heaven above, on the earth beneath, or in the waters below. You shall not bow down to them or worship them; for I, the Lord your God, am a jealous God, punishing the children for the sin of the fathers to the third and fourth generations of those who hate Me, but showing love to a thousand generations who love Me and keep My commandments.

The Creator was reminding the Hebrew slaves that they had experienced God because He delivered them from their slavery in Egypt. They already knew some truth about Him. Therefore, they needed to listen to and obey the Truth. On the other hand, believing what is not true by following false, made-up gods would mislead them back into slavery.

The First Commandment reminded the Hebrews that God is not an abstract principle or impersonal force. God is a personal Being, seeking to relate to human beings as precious persons made in His own image. Those who do not know the truth about God cannot know the truth about man. No wonder our Brahminical "saints" and "gurus" described most of our people as "low" caste.

Those who considered themselves "upper" castes did not allow our forefathers to build stone houses on the higher parts of the village. They forced us to live in mud homes in lower and vulnerable parts of the village. Our gurus did not know God; therefore, they did not know that every human being is made in God's image and has equal value and dignity.

The Second Commandment told the Hebrews to not make or worship idols. Phule spoke of the strong contrast with those priests that "read and reread hollow and ridiculous texts" that make us worship nature, idols, and demons. For, in doing so, they undermine our ability to govern nature. Development means harnessing and managing God-given natural resources for the good of human beings, animals, and nature. We are created to govern nature—not to worship it. The river is not God. As the Lord Jesus put it, "God is a Spirit, and those who worship Him must worship Him in truth and in Spirit."

Some politicians say that we will cease being backward if we vote for them, but Mahatma Phule knew that the first step in moving from backwardness to forwardness is becoming seekers and lovers of Truth.

Chapter Five

Why Didn't We
Develop Our Minds?

Our cultures made Khajuraho temples and Taj Mahals but did not make wheelbarrows for their slaves and backward castes. Why?

Several years ago, University of the Nations invited me to teach a course on community development in Uganda. I assumed that Uganda was poor because it was a resource-deprived desert. En route from Entebbe airport to Jinja, I saw hundreds of women and children carrying water on their heads. The sight made me feel at home because that is what women do in our villages and towns. It reinforced my assumptions about Africa's poverty, even though all I could see was lush greenery. The next day, my assumptions collapsed into confusion.

I discovered that my guest room was situated on the banks of Lake Victoria, one of the largest bodies of freshwater in the world, bigger than any lake in India. The mighty river Nile originates less than three miles from where I was staying. It starts with such force that, as early as 1954, the British began using its waters to generate hydroelectricity. Ever since then, Uganda has produced more power than it consumes. Some of it is sold to Kenya. That raised a puzzling question: With so much water and so much power, why were human beings carrying water on their heads?

Having lived in villages near Khajuraho in MP, I knew that this way of hauling water meant limited water in homes. People did not "waste" water to wash their hands, dishes, fruit, and vegetables adequately. Also, waterborne diseases gave them stomach diseases that sap energy and require otherwise avoidable treatment. The sight of women hauling water on their heads made me ask: Why don't Western women carry water on their heads? Why do some cultures do with their minds what the rest of us do with our muscles?

Could it be that the West uses the mind because the white race is more intelligent than us? No! The people living on the banks of the Nile were not dumb. They built the mighty pyramids thousands of years before the West learned how to make even small palaces. The problem is that our cultures made Khajuraho temples and Taj Mahals but did not make wheelbarrows for their slaves and backward castes. Why?

Historian Lynn White Jr.'s study, *Medieval Religion and Technology*, answered one side of my question. His pioneering research into the history of technology explained why the mediaeval West became the first civilization in history that did not rest on the backs of sweating slaves and oppressed castes. I was surprised to learn that European technology developed in its religious monasteries.

Why did European technology develop in monasteries?

Because the first chapter of the Bible taught Europe that God is a worker, not a meditator. In order to create our world, God worked for six days—so must we! To "work" is godly. The third chapter of the Bible taught that "toil" came as a curse upon human sin. Because of their sin, humans became the only species that had to eat of "the sweat of their brow." Since toil is a result of sin, spiritual salvation includes deliverance from sin as well as from toil—from mindless, repetitive labour that offers no choice. The monks who worked to develop technology were seeking God's glory as well as humanity's salvation.

In Khajuraho, our rulers and priests displayed great skills in building temples and other grand buildings for their prestige, pleasure, and enlightenment. In contrast, European monasteries began developing technologies that liberated powerless individuals from dehumanising slavery. They believed that toil—such as carrying water on your head morning and evening 365 days a year— is dehumanising because it forces a human being to do what can be done by an ox, a horse, wind, water, wheels, or electricity.

Our monks and sages were no less intelligent than European monks. The philosophies they constructed, the caves that they sculpted, and the temples that they built testify that they were second to none in imagination, ingenuity, architecture, engineering, discipline, and organisation. In fact, our monks shared a problem in common with European monks: none of them had a wife to haul water, grind wheat, or find fuel for cooking bread. One difference was that our religious tradition, especially the Buddha, required monks to beg for food, while the Bible said that whoever does not work should not eat. European monks invented machines because they had to bring their own water, clean their own latrines, grind their own wheat, and bake their own bread. They developed technologies because their religious requirement to work was coupled with

- Spiritual quest for salvation from sin and its consequences, including toil,

- theological commitment to the dignity of every human being—male or female, high or low—and more importantly,

- religious obligation to cultivate the human mind.

As religious institutions, European monasteries were unique; some of them evolved into universities because they were created to cultivate the mind as much as character. They made a distinction between myth and truth and believed that the human mind could know the truth. Therefore, they required monks to study logic, philosophy, rhetoric, languages, literature, law, mathematics, music, agriculture, and metallurgy in addition to the Scriptures. These religious institutions became the nursery of rational disciplines such as medicine and music, law and technology, astronomy and botany, economics, and morality. European monasteries cultivated the mind because they were founded upon St. Augustine's exposition of the Bible, which taught that the human mind is not an evolved version of the animal brain but qualitatively different, made in the Creator's image. They did not think that the mind is a product of blind chance or Primeval Ignorance (Avidya). They believed that the human mind can know God, goodness, and beauty; that human words can communicate truth because God has made our minds in his image; and that God gave us the gift of language so that He might communicate with us, His children. The biblical worldview propelled these monasteries to begin creating a uniquely *rational* religious man who became capable of developing complex theories that created rapidly growing economies and institutions that produced civil societies where power was subject to agreed-upon principles.

Given the fact that civilization came to India and China centuries before Europe, we should have been aeons ahead of the West in developing technology and economy. Why did we fall behind? The answer is that our cultures were shaped by worldviews that taught us that intellect was our problem and salvation depended not on deliverance from sin but on deliverance from the intellect.

In 1974, I spent some time in Rishikesh at the ashram of the late Maharishi Mahesh Yogi, the founder of Transcendental Meditation (TM). The world-famous British pop group, The Beatles, helped him build this beautiful ashram on the banks of the River Ganga, where it comes down to the plains from the Himalayas. The president of the Indian branch of his movement initiated me into TM in the Maharishi's own living room. He gave me a mantra: the name of a minor demigod. He asked me to recite this sound silently for twenty minutes, twice a day. In advanced stages, he said, I would need to fast and recite that mantra for several hours at a time.

I asked the initiator what my mantra meant. He told me not to bother with its meaning. The principle of Transcendental Meditation is not to know truth but to empty one's mind of all rational thought—to "transcend" thinking. To think is to remain in ignorance, in bondage to rational thought. Meditation, he explained, is a means of escaping thinking by focusing attention on a sacred, though meaningless, sound like *Om*.

His explanation helped me understand why our monks did not develop technology, universities, and science. Of course, Indian sages did not lack intelligence. Many of them excelled at philosophy, medicine, mathematics, the arts, and sculpture. Some of them did build what we now call "universities" in Nalanda and Taxila. Yet, none of this created in India a rational civilization because, in spite of their great intelligence, our sages considered the rational act of reading and thinking about the meaning of the words and text a hindrance to mystical enlightenment. Their idea of meditation was the opposite of the Western or biblical idea of meditation; they believed that salvation comes from emptying our minds of all thoughts and words. This philosophical dilemma continues to haunt the Maharishi International University, founded by the Maharishi Mahesh Yogi and already downgraded to the Maharishi University of Management.

As I have discussed in *The Book That Made Your World: How the Bible Created the Soul of Western Civilization* (Thomas Nelson, 2012), our monks did not develop liberating music, technology, or science because they did not use their minds to replace muscles; they tried hard not to think—and they succeeded. Our sages and "forward" castes did not build schools, colleges, and universities for us because their religious worldview did not require them to cultivate the mind. It encouraged our sadhus to intake hallucinogenic drugs such as ganja and bhang and to meditate—preferably with their heads literally buried in sand.

We have a bigger tragedy today: Now we do have schools, but many of our people still send their children to haul water or collect cow dung instead of enabling them to cultivate their minds. Too many of our people still don't believe that in order to be God-like, we have to cultivate our minds.

Chapter Six
Beyond Reservations and Politics

India is an ancient civilisation. We have had great philosophers. Why then are 750 million Indians "educationally" backward?

President Barack Obama's visit to India (6-8 November 2010) proved one thing: The world now knows that India need not be backward. However, it is quite possible for India to move forward while the vast majority of OBCs and other "backward" groups remain backward.

Take, for example, Gurcharan Kurmi. That is not his real name, but he lives in a village in district Panna, Madhya Pradesh. Twelve years ago, he graduated from a government college but never found a job. His parents and brothers exempt him from working on the farm. Instead, they fed him, his wife, and his child so that he would be free to study. He earned nothing, but his family bought him the best boots, bicycles, books, bags, and everything else he needed to go to college. His graduation made them so proud that they took loans to enable him to spend years searching for jobs in neighbouring Satna and faraway Delhi. His family had no connections in these cities that could help him find a job. The quality of his education did not enable him to compete with students who went to English-medium schools. So, he never found anything that would pay him enough to bring his wife and child to a room in the city and repay his parents' debt. Illiterate folk who slept on the streets in Delhi and worked as labourers did better than him, financially. His college degree made it hard for him to follow their example. His frustrations so discouraged other families that they are now reluctant to send their children to college. Neighbours describe Gurcharan's situation in this popular idiom: *Dhobi ka kutta, na ghar ka na ghat ka* (A washerman's dog is good neither as a watchdog nor for carrying laundry as a pack mule.)

In 1979, Justice B. P. Mandal was appointed to determine which castes were backward "educationally and socially" but had not been included in the Simon Commission's Schedule of Untouchable Castes (1930). In 1990, Mr. V. P. Singh, then our prime minister, agreed to reserve special quotas for these Other Backward Classes (OBCs) in educational institutions and government jobs. The intention was to make it possible for young people like Gurcharan to study and work in the non-agricultural sectors of the economy. But the idea is not working too well.

Unable to find a job, Gurcharan also spent a few years helping to organise the Bahujan Samaj Party (BSP) in his region. He believed in Manyawar Kanshi Ram's slogan, "Politics is the key that opens every lock." It took him several years to realise that his political work opened all sorts of doors for people with power and some doors for those who became slaves of the powerful, but few doors for others such as him. Political activism, at least in his experience, impoverished those who volunteered their time at their family's expense. These harsh realities had robbed Gurcharan of all hope when I first met him in Haridwar. He had begun to wonder if backwardness was his fate—if it had something to do with his karma, his caste, or his horoscope.

It took many hours of discussion for Gurcharan to understand that our collective backwardness is a result of our religious culture. For example, we discussed the question of educational backwardness: India is an ancient civilization. We have had great philosophers. Why then are 750 million Indians "educationally" backward? Should our people study only if jobs are guaranteed? Why can't enough of us become entrepreneurs who create jobs for others?

My questions shocked Gurcharan:

- Should jobs be our primary motivation for learning?
- Or should we study to seek truth?

- When, for thousands of years, learned sages have established great ashrams in Haridwar, why didn't a single guru establish one university to educate backward castes to become entrepreneurs?

Gurcharan began to understand my point when we visited the magnificent ashram of Swami Dayanand, one of the most brilliant gurus in Haridwar. Swamiji explained to us that Hinduism uses logic to destroy logic. Why? Because, according to Swamiji, logic and rationality keep us in bondage, in ignorance. Thinking does not lead to Enlightenment. Samadhi is the answer, which is achieved by meditation that silences our minds and transcends all thoughts. A university is an institution to cultivate your mind; an ashram is a retreat to get rid of your mind.

What helped Gurcharan most was reading a little book by Acharya Rajneesh. It is called *Beyond and Beyond*. This book was published in 1970, before Rajneesh became a Bhagwan and then Osho. Gurcharan knew that Rajneesh began his public life as a professor of philosophy in the university at Sagar, MP. What Gurcharan did not know was that Rajneesh lost interest in philosophy and the university when he understood Indian philosophy. In this little book with a mystical sounding title, Rajneesh teaches one of the most important lessons that he learned from the Buddha. That is, the mind or the intellect is humanity's most fundamental problem. The little book is peppered with statements such as, "Intellect is the chief villain," "Do not use your mind," and "Learn the techniques of killing the mind." "Religion," Rajneesh agrees with Swami

Dayanand, "is a process to go beyond thinking, to achieve a point in your mind where there is no thinking at all." This view of human rationality was an important reason why our gurus did not build universities to educate our people.

In contrast, monks in Western countries started turning some of their monasteries into universities one thousand years ago. This was because one of the most influential church fathers, St. Augustine (AD 354–430) explained to the Roman world the Bible's teaching on the human mind. He explained that, according to the Bible, the mind is not the source of ignorance but one of the Creator's greatest gifts to us. Our minds are made in the image of God so that we may love Him, become like Him, understand His creation, and manage it as His children. This divine mandate required monks to study science and develop technology. Augustine wrote,

> Far be it from us to suppose that God abhors in us that [the intellect] by virtue of which He has made us superior to other animals. Far be it, I say, that we should believe in such a way as to exclude the necessity either of accepting or requiring reason, since we could not even believe unless we possessed rational souls.

Deeply religious leaders began to reform Europe in the sixteenth century. They required everyone to study—not to get a job, but to know God. If our minds are made in God's image, then to become godly means to cultivate our minds.

While our religious culture condemned us to educational backwardness, the revival of a different religion lifted a small nation such as England out of poverty. Nation-wide revivals of biblical spirituality went on to impact other English-speaking nations, such as President Obama's nation, America. University of Hawaii emeritus professor of history Cedric B. Cowing studied the impact of the eighteenth-century biblical "Revival" in England and the "Great Awakening" in America, which is also called "New Light." He came to the conclusion that these religious revivals played the most significant role in lifting these nations out of ignorance and poverty. Religion gave them the actual skills they needed to succeed economically. In his book, *The Great Awakening and the American Revolution*, Cowing wrote,

> In Britain, many of the converts of [revival leaders] Whitefield and Wesley were motivated to learn to read and write. In the northern colonies [in America]... the energies and discipline released by the New Light were the inspiration needed to master abstract religious material. In comprehending theological as well

as devotional printed matter, the emotions aided the development of cognitive skills. The novices in focusing on the stages of conversion were studying a process analogous to the still mysterious secular sequence of gathering data, altering hypotheses, and somehow relying upon intuition to synthesise the conclusions. This type of thinking would have a more general utility later. The Great Awakening induced a grass-roots intellectualism that ultimately spread in every direction, from belief in God's sovereignty all the way to agnosticism." (Cedric B. Cowing, The Great Awakening and the American Revolution: Colonial Thought in the 18th Century, Chicago: Rand McNally, 1971, p. 72).

How did these mass spiritual awakenings lift those countries out of the poverty that is chronic for Gurcharan and so many of our people?

In his famous Inquiry into the wealth of the nations, Adam Smith noted that hard work by itself does not result in prosperity. Gurcharan's family works hard, as do primitive tribes that hunt and gather the whole day, seven days a week. Why is their life still so hard? The difference between poverty and prosperity is determined by how much "skill, dexterity, and judgement" (in short, thought) is put into work.

Letting one's mind direct one's muscles involves many things. Technology is one of them. The rational use and organisation of time, labour, available resources, and capital are equally important. Proper relationships among all participants in an economic system and reasonable sharing of resources, costs, and profits make vital differences to the economic life of a people. These economic relationships are expressed in sensible principles, laws, contracts, taxes, and legal and financial institutions. Some of the principles and laws of any good society are written down, while others are taken for granted because they are a part of their religious culture and its philosophical ethos. A religious culture that privileges a tiny section (the upper castes) over the majority of people (the Bahujans in India) can never ensure all-encompassing growth for all the citizens of a country. Gurcharan's college degree alone will not help him advance in life. A change is needed in the entire culture, where sensible principles are applicable for the progress of all.

President Obama knows that there is no reason why India cannot become greater than America. The key that will unlock the potential of our people is the kind of religious, cultural, and socio-political revival that transformed England and America.

Chapter Seven
Reservations
Political Engineering Versus Social Transformation

Democracy is "freedom," but in order to use that freedom, the powerless have to develop their latent capacity by fighting, losing, and learning.

Our reservations policy did not make Mayawati the chief minister of UP. Her mentor, Manyawar Kanshi Ramji, condemned "reservations" as the source of the Chamcha Age—the Era of Stooges. In his helpful book, *The Chamcha Age*, Kanshi Ram argued that the British Raj produced men like Babasaheb Dr. Bhimrao Ambedkar who were genuine leaders of India's oppressed. They had the inner strength to stand up to giants, including the British as well as Mahatma Gandhi. Democratic freedom should have produced many more leaders like them, but it didn't—at least not during the first four decades.

The reservation system in politics, argued Kanshi Ramji, gives to the Scheduled Castes only stooges as MPs and MLAS. They crawl at the feet of upper-caste netas to get tickets to Parliament. After being elected, they serve the interests of the upper castes, not the downtrodden. That makes them chamchas, not leaders.

In other words, reserving seats for SC and ST candidates corrupts democracy. Political reservations prevent the oppressed majority (Bahujan) from acquiring real political power. That is why Kanshi Ram insisted that the best way for the Bahujan to obtain democratic power is to compete against the upper castes in non-reserved seats.

In 1991, the Rewa Parliamentary Constituency gave Manyawar Kanshi Ram the opportunity to prove his thesis. I was sitting with him in his bungalow in New Delhi when Rewa's collector called on a private line. He urged Kanshi Ramji to run for Parliament from Rewa. The collector said that each one of the five major parties, including the Congress, Janata Dal, BIP, and the Communist Party, was putting up Brahmins as their candidates for Parliament. Therefore, any competent non-Brahmin would easily win the election.

Kanshi Ram gave the BSP ticket to my friend Sri Bhim Singh Patel, who won exactly as the collector had predicted. BSP's victory proved the point that the downtrodden do not need the upper castes' charity. Democracy is "freedom," but in order to use that freedom, the powerless have to develop their latent capacity by fighting, losing, and learning.

As a philosophical idea, democracy is antithetical to the Hindu belief that some castes are born to rule because of their good karma in a past life, while the others are born to serve due to their bad karma. Democracy assumes equality and freedom for every individual. When Mayawati won, she proved that karma is not merely a false religious doctrine; it is an evil idea that has sustained India's hierarchical social system and served the interests of the upper castes.

Caste system is one example of "social engineering." Like apartheid in South Africa or racial segregation in America earlier in history, any caste system separates neighbours from neighbours along ethnic lines. Self-appointed "wise men" determine every child's destiny by putting a future Phule or Ambedkar, Mulayam or Mayawati in occupational boxes, thus limiting their God-given talents.

Other failed examples of social engineering include Communism, Nazism, and also (in a milder way) the reservations system. Some of these officially engineered systems seek social justice by treating people as bricks and mortar. In the worst cases, they put human beings in social boxes according to some wise man's ideas. A fundamental problem with reservations is that one cannot take the benefit without the stigma. For example, in order to get your child admitted into an educational institution, you have to label her or him "backward"—unequal with the rest of his/ her class.

Had Kanshi Ram been content with reservations, Mayawati's highest goal would have been to become another Jagjivan Ram. Without reservations, she has the chance to be our prime minister. She could have had that honour, had she supported Mulayam Singhji to remain UP's chief minister, and focused her energies on enthroning her friends as chief ministers of MP, Punjab, Delhi, Rajasthan, Haryana, and Bihar. She missed Delhi only because she kept her eyes focused on Lucknow. Historian Paul Johnson's book, *Modern Times*, is a classic study that concludes that, as a concept, social engineering was the greatest evil of the twentieth century. Yet, it is not surprising that it continues to be popular, even though it is a proven failure. It appeals because it sells itself as "social justice." It attracts a following, because

> 1. It is more effort for the people themselves to try to eradicate social wrongs, and easier for the people to simply give to the government the responsibility to address social wrongs, and

> 2. Championing a policy of reservations makes it easy for politicians to gather votes by pretending to be the saviours of the masses.

Moreover, the upper castes oppose reservations because of their own shortsighted self-interest, without proposing practical solutions to the real problems of the majority of India, which is still desperately poor. Mayawati's conquest of Lucknow in 2007 was stunning, even if it was a poor and temporary example of social transformation. She forced the Brahmins to accept a Chamar as their leader. Her victory would have been a great example of social transformation had the upper castes in UP genuinely repented of their false beliefs about karma and inequality and consequent treatment of their neighbours as inferiors to themselves. Without such a fundamental change of mind and heart, it is safe to suspect that they will use Mayawati for their own ends and, when possible, abandon her to recapture power.

Of course, Brahmins have the right to fight and win Lucknow; yet they also have the responsibility to love their neighbours as themselves, because the truth is that all human beings are created equal and endowed by their Creator with the dignity of being made in God's own image. In contrast to social engineering, *social transformation* changes society by changing its fundamental beliefs and values. Social engineering does not produce real and enduring change, but social transformation does produce change that is genuine and lasting.

Kanshi Ram did not believe in reservations, yet he launched what was one of the longest and least-reported political agitations in Indian history. For months on end, every single day, BSP activists gathered near the Parliament in New Delhi, courted arrest, and asked the then prime minister V. P. Singh, "*Mandal Commission Lagu Karo, Varna Kursi Khali Karo,*" Implement the (reservations for OBCs recommended by the) Mandal Commission or vacate the prime minister's chair.

I played a small role in starting this. I got a copy of the Janata Dal's election manifesto from 7 Jantar Mantar and highlighted the sections that promised to implement the Mandal Commission's Report and allow Scheduled Castes to convert to Buddhism and Sikhism. As Kanshi Ramji was preparing his speech for our massive rally in Ramlila Grounds in Delhi, I gave the manifesto to him, specifically pointing out some of these promises that the Janata Dal had made. Kanshi Ramji held up that manifesto during the rally, read those highlighted sections, and addressed V. P. Singh directly: "Reservations is not our method. It is your (socialist) idea. Therefore, we will hold you accountable to your promises. Implement Mandal Commission or quit.

Kanshi Ramji didn't think that V. P. Singh would do what Indira Gandhi had not done, because Kanshi Ramji didn't know that George Fernandes had been opening V. P. Singh's mind for Lohia's socialist writings. Chaudhary Devi Lal's plan to pull down V. P. Singh's government forced V. P. Singh into adopting reservations as a way of appearing to be the OBC's champion. I am mentioning these titbits of history simply to make the point that it is naïve to believe politicians simply because they say what we want to hear.

Kanshi Ramji championed the Mandal Commission's recommendation for reservations to woo OBC votes, not because he believed in social engineering. Likewise, V. P. Singh presented himself as an OBC Messiah, only to retain the PM's kursi. Neither of them actually believed in reservations, but their problem was that the socialists believed in social engineering and had taught the Bahujan that reservations equal social justice.

Nevertheless, it is significant to remember that even the Socialists did not talk about reservations in the private sector of the economy. They didn't because the "free" market economy, or capitalism, does not fit into their theory of a state-controlled economy. The free market is the opposite of a socialist or government-controlled economic system.

No sane person will dispute that the Hindu socio-economic system has been unjust and iniquitous. It has condemned the vast majority of Indians to backwardness. The question is: Do the backward castes need social engineering, or do they rather need spiritual, intellectual, political, and economic opportunity? Economic freedom means that the government should meddle with the economy as little as absolutely necessary. A business should be free to hire and fire employees in light of what is good for the business. It is in an employer's interest to hire the best available people and do all that it can to keep the best workers. Only a foolish employer will refuse to hire a good backward-caste employee simply because of his caste, and it is also unwise to work for any employer who has such foolish attitudes. The larger question is: Can India compete and win internationally if we demand reservations, whether business or in our national cricket or Olympic teams?

More than reservations in the private sector, what the Bahujan need is good education and training. The government can run a few good institutions, but it is foolish to expect the government to improve most public schools. If a community wants great education for its children, then it has to organise itself to meet that need.

Among other things, religion is a means of organising a

community. The caste system organised us only to deny education to the Bahujan. But the guilt does not rest on Hinduism alone. Buddhism rejected the Brahminical monopoly of priesthood, but it had little interest in cultivating the minds of the masses because it did not believe that the human intellect (buddhi) could know the truth.

Mass literacy was a Jewish idea. About 3,500 years ago, the Israelites were slaves in Egypt. Therefore, most of them were literate, oral learners. Education was preserved as the privilege of the elite. Individuals, such as Moses, who happened to have grown up in Pharaoh's palace, were exceptions. However, when the Jews (then called Hebrews) came out of slavery, God gave them the Ten Commandments in what is called by them "the Law"—that is, the Five Books of Moses (the first five books of the Bible). God commanded Moses to "write" the Law for these oral learners. Since God had written the Law, it became necessary for the Jews to learn to read and write, to write important parts of that law in their homes and door posts, to meditate upon God's word, and thus to cultivate their minds and their souls. The Jewish temples and synagogues therefore, became the centres both of worship as well as of learning. Because Christianity was born in that Jewish milieu, many versions of Christianity saw education as an integral aspect of Christian missions. That is why in Kerala, the most literate state in mainland India, the word for school, pallikudam, literally means the "building next to the church." So, whether the school belongs to the (communist-ruled) state or to the Hindu community, in Kerala it is still called "the building next to the church."

Because the Lord Jesus himself commanded his disciples to go and teach, the real blame for the continuing educational backwardness of the Bahujan rests upon the Christian church. I knew one American missionary lady who managed the only English-medium school in her district. She made it a practice of interviewing parents in order to admit children to her school. This kept the poor and illiterate children out of the best school in the area. The upper-caste parents came with recommendations of local Christians and were admitted.

The school had over four hundred students and only one Dalit—the grandson of the school's gardener. This was not a financial issue, since Compassion International had been giving scholarships to about seventy children. Every scholarship, except one, went to an uppercaste child.

Why would an American missionary act this way? My explanation is that her eyes had been so blinded by the racism of American culture, that she had no difficulty in compromising with the evils of our casteist social system.

What missionaries like her did to the Bahujan was bad enough; what is happening now is utterly foolish... Some American missions are teaching Indian Christian leaders to not give literacy to illiterate, oral learners. This is, of course, no place to explain and answer this stupidity. It is sufficient to note that, thankfully, the Indian church has enough leaders now who are able to stand up against the follies of some American missions. Be that as it may, the important need is for the Bahujan to be fooled neither by religious nor political leaders, but determine carefully what is good for them and for India, and to work for that.

PART III

ENSLAVING MYTHS

Chapter Eight
History Can Transform, Myths Will Manipulate

Why would devotees donate hundreds of millions of rupees annually for the privilege of worshipping a penis, whether made of ice or stone? The power is in the myth.

Every Indian's heart should bleed for Kashmir. As I write this article (in July 2010) innocent blood is once again flowing on the streets of Srinagar, taking the total number of casualties (civilians, militants, and Armed Forces) to around 80,000 since 1988. Families are desperate; many had borrowed money to get ready to serve the anticipated 350,000 tourists. They were looking forward to earning honest money, repaying their debts, and moving one step forward by investing surplus income in their homes and businesses. Instead, streets are deserted; houseboats are empty; enraged locals are indoors; while a few of their neighbours battle 500,000 Indian soldiers. Everyone is mourning the fact that the state is moving backwards.

In June 2010, I was in Srinagar when the tourist season for that year began. Among other engagements, I gave a lecture at the university's postgraduate department of business management on the question Does Hindu Capitalism Have a Future? Bollywood could have made Kashmir its number one destination for outdoor filming. That alone would have drawn all the capitalists that my students would want to meet. But given what we have done to keep Kashmir backward, Bollywood invests much of its black money abroad.

In Srinagar, my most moving encounter was with Mr. Verma. I was climbing up the steep steps of the 1,000-foot-high Shiva Temple, the most spectacular "High Place" in Srinagar. It is called Takht-e-Suleiman (The Throne of Solomon). Mr. Verma, an average educated businessman, was coming down. Yet, he stopped to catch his breath. Clutching his heart with his right hand, he explained his embarrassment: "I do not have one lung. Your lung holds your heart; but my heart is hanging. Therefore, I am not allowed to climb steps. I had to go up this hill because they say that you will not earn all the available merit from this pilgrimage unless you pay homage at this shrine. I want better karma for my next life. Therefore, I had to ignore my cardiologist and take this risk."

I could not help but respect Mr. Verma's deep devotion. But, to be honest, I was also furious at the myths that enslave our people. Takht-e-Suleiman is magnificent. A revolving restaurant on top along with ski facilities for winter would bring all the tourists Srinagar wants. That brief encounter with Mr. Verma explained why most of Kashmir Valley had renounced Hinduism and converted to Islam by the seventeenth century. The Shiva Temple became a sideshow a century ago when a Muslim shepherd discovered the 60-foot-long, 30-foot-wide, and 15-foot-high Amarkantak cave 12,729 feet above sea level. The cave, about eighty-six miles northeast of Srinagar, is now the prime pilgrimage site where our people go to worship the Shivling (Shiva's penis), made of natural ice. The penis "pulsates." Every month it increases and decreases in size, apparently following the monthly cycle of the moon.

Why would devotees donate hundreds of millions of rupees annually for the privilege of worshipping a penis, whether made of ice or stone? The power is in the myth.

Lord Shiva is an eternal Brahmachari (celibate) and, therefore, does not have a wife. Parvati is his "consort" or sex-partner who helps awaken his enormous sexual energy called Kundalini, symbolised by hooded cobras. Sitting in this cave, Parvati urged Shiva to explain why she had to die while he was immortal (*Amar*). Shiva said that the story of immortality is too long to relate. But Parvati sat down, determined to listen. Shiva closed his eyes in meditation and summoned the demon Kalagni Rudra. He ordered the demon to burn up all living things within audible distance to ensure that one hears the secret of immortality.

The story was really long, but Parvati kept saying "hun" (yes) until she fell asleep. A parrot appeared from under Shiva and began to mimic Parvati's "hun." When Shiva opened his eyes, he asked Parvati if she now knew the secret of immortality. "No," she said, "I fell asleep."

Who then was saying "hun?" Shiva was enraged at the prospect that someone mortal may have heard the secret reserved for gods. The parrot realised that he was in trouble and flew off. As Shiva chased the parrot, it found the wife of Vyasdev sitting at the entrance of her cottage with her "mouth" open. The parrot flew into her, and she became pregnant. She gave birth to Shukradev, who was born with the knowledge of the secret of immortality.

The sages gathered around Shukradev. They flattered and pressed him to tell them the secret. Once he agreed, the gods became extremely nervous. They urged Shiva to prevent Shukradev from this reckless act of revelation. Shiva too was angry, but how could he kill someone who received the secret of immortality from Shiva himself? The best that Shiva could do was to put a curse: "No one who hears the secret will become immortal. He will only enter Shivlok—the realm of Shiva's (sexual) bliss."

I did see the inside of the temple, but decided to sit outside, on the "Throne of Solomon" and meditate as I took in the breathtaking beauty. I didn't need a guru to explain the myth.

It takes no intelligence to understand the "parrot" that came from below Shiva and made his neighbour's wife pregnant through her "mouth.".

Nor does it take much to understand why our Brahmacharis, who have renounced their own wives, want their neighbours' wives to worship the male sexual organ.

It suits husbands to take their wives to the temple to learn to worship their male organs. Otherwise, they may have to pay therapists to teach their wives to arouse their Kundalini Shakti (serpent power or sexual energy).

The puzzle that I wanted to figure out was: Why is this "High Place" called the Throne of Solomon?

It is of course possible that the mountain is named after a local Muslim nobleman called Suleiman. But history records no such nobleman; also, the High Place has had that name since before Islam came into existence. Is it then possible that some Jews travelled up the Silk Route and settled in that beautiful valley, naming that mountain after one of their most famous kings? Against the commands of God, Solomon had also made shrines for his wives who worshipped other gods through fertility cults. The theory that some inhabitants of Kashmir were originally Jews is a strong possibility. The Bible records that after Israel split into two nations, the ten northern tribes of Israel forsook the living God who had delivered them from their slavery in Egypt and commanded them not to make idols. The Israelites disobeyed their Saviour-God and began to install sacred stones on "high places. They institutionalised shrine prostitutes, both male and female, and worshipped demons to the point of sacrificing their own children to these demonic gods.

God's prophets warned Israel against these sins of idolatry and adultery. When the nation refused to listen to their living God, He destroyed their entire nation. He sent them into slavery in Assyria (Western Iraq). That is not far from the start of the Silk Route, which could have brought the Jews into Kashmir. Scholars have, for a long time, pointed out similarities between Saivism and corrupted versions of Jewish monotheism, but that is not relevant to our discussion. The question is: Could myths that inspire people to worship Shiva's penis condemn a people to bondage and backwardness?

One of my favourite uncles, Chachaji, worked as an engineer for the Indian Railways. Once, he had to spend several weeks repairing a bridge in a jungle in Bihar. I was about fourteen when my "aunt" (Chachiji), took me to spend a weekend with her husband, who was camping in a remote Forest Guest House. Even though they had been married for several years, they did not have any children.

On the second morning, while they were still in their room, I went out to enjoy the forest. I saw a man bring in a Shivling and set it up in an empty room, which was quickly turned into a temporary shrine. Later in the morning, I was told that I had to stay away from that area because a Tantrik was coming to treat Chachiji so that she could have babies.

The treatment worked. Nine months later, she gave birth to two boys. When the boys became teenagers and needed their father, Chachaji took the vow of brahmacharya (celibacy), abandoned his family, and became a guru. A few women and couples started coming to him seeking Enlightenment or at least Shivlok by awakening their Serpent Power (Kundalini). Initially, the Hindus of Kashmir had good reasons for rejecting such destructive myths in favour of the simplicity of Islam. Whether or not their conversion liberated them is another—and legitimate—question.

Mahatma Jotirao Phule, the pioneer of the lower-caste social reform movement, understood how myth makers had enslaved India's women and backward castes. He tried to understand what liberated the women and the backward castes of Europe and America. When he realised that Europe and America moved forward because the Messiah and his followers unleashed the power of Truth, Phule urged the Shudras to become Truth-seekers.

Chapter Nine
Who Is Afraid of Liberty?

Manipulative myths that serve the priests' interests require force for their survival.

On 7 August 2010, some "devout" Muslims in Badakhshan, Afghanistan, dragged ten Christians out of their vehicle, robbed them, and shot them one by one. The victims of this brutal "spirituality" included three women. They were returning from mountainous Nuristan after completing an eye-camp for poor Muslims. The women had joined the medical team to make it possible for their Muslim counterparts to receive treatment without having to see a male doctor, nurse, or translator. They were "guilty" of walking miles and miles in hilly terrain, and offering free treatment and surgery to those who suffered from various eye diseases.

The murderers did not blame their victims for converting Muslims, because everyone knew that they did not convert anyone. The Christians were blamed for simply carrying their Persian Bibles with them! In actual fact, it was their Christ-like, self-sacrificing service that was seen as a serious threat to Islam.

I knew two of the victims—Dan Terry and Tom Little. They were the team leaders. Our daughters studied with theirs, and for two years their families lived next door to ours. I talked more with Dan because he was more talkative. Dan, 64, first went to serve Afghanistan in 1971, long before the Soviet invasion or the Taliban takeover. Their organisation, International Assistance Mission (IAM), was registered with the Afghan government as a Christian group. It had signed the "Principles of Conduct for the International Red Cross and Red Crescent Movement and NGOs in Disaster

Response Programmes." One of these "principles" stipulates that aid will not be used to further a particular political or religious standpoint. IAM was strict about following the "No Preaching" policy. That is why many Muslims invited them to their towns and villages and protected them. The team travelled unarmed and without security. Why would devout Muslims fear such dedicated public servants?

Dan explained the puzzle to me: "We do not preach," he said, "but everyone knows that we serve because we follow Christ. Therefore, many intelligent Afghans come to us privately and say, 'Our land is under a curse—the curse of Islam. We want freedom to seek truth. But we are kept in bondage at gunpoint."

Opposition to Truth Seeking:

So, why does Islam deny individuals the freedom to seek and find truth?

It is because Islam is not a public truth like the Gospel of Jesus Christ, whose death and resurrection had many eyewitnesses. The Gospel is not a private religious revelation; many people saw Jesus die for our sin and rise again. In contrast, Islam is based on the private revelations of an individual. Private revelations cannot be cross-examined; if questioned, they have to be enforced.

If that is the reason for "Islamic enforcement," why is Hindutva scared of giving individuals the freedom to investigate truth and choose their own religious or non-religious beliefs? Why does it see individual liberty as a grave political threat to its existence?

Through an advertisement in *Hindustan Times* (27 July 2010, Page 4), the Law Commission of the Government of India notified the public that it is, or at least was, considering a national law about religious conversion. Some people suspect that the legislation under consideration may be a subtle avatar of the law that was first proposed in the late 1970s, during Morarji Desai's rule, to restrict an Indian individual's freedom to choose his or her faith. The commission, however, says that its primary reason for considering this legislation is a formal request by the Kerala High Court, which has found it difficult to resolve divorce cases that involve inter-religious marriages. For example, if a Hindu marries a Muslim, should the divorce be according to the Hindu Marriage Act or the Muslim Marriage Act? The High Court feels that resolving such cases will be simplified if one of the spouses "legally" converts to another's faith. The problem is that, in the social realities of India, requiring truth seekers to file legal papers declaring their new faith can endanger their businesses, inheritance, and even life. If a Brahmin woman files legal papers that she has become a Muslim, Hindutva forces might even start a riot. So, the Kerala High Court's suggestion may solve a few technical problems in a private case, but it will create umpteen public problems.

The truth behind myths:

Why is Hindutva so opposed to liberty?

I understood Hindutva's problem during a winter vacation in Tamil Nadu. We were visiting the world-famous Meenakshi temple in Madurai. Our guide was enjoying lecturing to our group. Our host, the principal of a local woman's college and her daughter, had accompanied my wife, our young (minor) daughters, and me. After learning much about the grandeur of ancient Hindu religion, culture, and architecture, I asked the guide, "Isn't this a tantric temple? Isn't this a platform where sexual orgies would have happened in the holy temple?"

The guide blushed and took me away from the ladies. He began to point out the erotic mini sculptures that are easy to miss seeing in that huge temple complex. "This temple had bigger and better erotic sculptures than Khajuraho," said the guide, "but they have been vandalised and stolen. Yes, that platform is where the priests and royalty had sexual orgies with devadasis (female "slaves of gods").

I left the temple saying to myself, "Indian women have such a strong sense of modesty: How did these brahmacharis (celibate priests) get the women to have sex with them in public?"

From Madurai, we went to Madras (now Chennai) to see the famous Mylapore temple. Before we got off the bus, the guide told us the story behind the temple: "Shiva and Parvati were sitting here. A peacock came, and Parvati got distracted. Shiva was angry and cursed Parvati. Immediately, she became a peacock. She was terrified and began to worship the Shivling morning and evening, until Shiva was pleased and turned her back into a woman."

"What a crazy story!" was my spontaneous reaction. "Why would anyone build such a magnificent temple to commemorate such an absurd story?"

As it happened, I was using that winter vacation to read the Greek philosopher Plato's famous book *The Republic*. On the way from Madurai, I had been reading the section where Plato proposes that philosopher kings (Brahmins in our context) should not marry. Why? Because wives want to have babies and then they nag you, demanding time, attention, and energy to bring up those babies! Philosopher kings shouldn't have to bother with crying, messy babies that want to be cuddled! Therefore, philosopher-kings should have a community of wives. The best women should be reserved for their use, but the children produced should be brought up by nurses and teachers paid for by the Republic.

Plato's proposal has attracted many. The problem, however, is this—why would a woman give herself to someone who makes no long-term commitment to love her and take care of her? Plato's solution was that philosophers should invent religious stories (myths) that motivate women to have sex with them. In other words, a clever leader (religious and political) should make no commitment to love a woman and take responsibility to nurture their children; he should invent religious stories to manipulate her into pleasing him. On a printed page, Plato's proposal was nothing more than a cold, abstract, rational paragraph that failed to grab my attention. But the story behind the temple had made it alive. The Mylapore temple was also a tantric temple. Tantra was the state religion in most Hindu states. The temple was built to manipulate women to worship the penis. The main temple had fallen down in the nineteenth century, and much of the present temple was rebuilt without erotic sculptures, because under Muslim and European influence, Tantra had gone underground.

Myths are no better than private revelations. They cannot be cross-examined and judged to be true or untrue. Manipulative myths that serve the priests' interests require force for their survival. Plato denounced democracy as the worst of all political systems. He felt that philosopher-kings (Brahmins) must rule, and they should not give to the masses, to slaves, or to women the right to question their motives or myths. Plato's disciple, Aristotle, trained Alexander the Great to be a philosopher-king, who became one of history's most ruthless tyrants. All his life, Alexander enjoyed the company and advice of philosophers!

Only truth can be genuinely tolerant:

Democracy is dangerous. It gives "little" individuals the freedom to question and discard manipulative religious myths perpetrated and perpetuated by "big" philosophers and thinkers. Mahatma Jotirao Phule said that we are backward because a vast majority of the Shudras have not yet become Truth-seekers. They have not become thoughtful people with courage to question the manipulative myths of our Brahmin priests, and to discard myths in favour of truth.

Truth is tolerant because it is not afraid of free and serious examination. Truth sets us free. That is why the living God invited the Hebrews and all people to seek and find Him. He told them not to allow their leaders to make false gods for them. Idols with their supporting myths are created to enslave and exploit.

Those whose power comes from false gods are afraid of liberty... and they should be. Therefore, the Law Commission and the Government of India should not use the pretext of addressing some exception to the general rule—for example, divorce by an interfaith couple—to abridge or abrogate our fundamental freedoms, which are enshrined in the Indian Constitution, to believe, practice, and propagate whatever we see to be the truth. May India live up to Mahatma Phule's personal motto, which is now also our national motto—Satyameva Jayate! Truth Alone Triumphs!

Chapter Ten
Haiti's Disaster and Hollywood's
Avatar Lessons for India

The spirits of trees and rivers, astrology and mythology, do not save us from our sin. They enslave individuals and whole nations in fear, superstition, and corruption.

Most of the nine million people of Haiti are of African descent. They live in approximately 10,000 square miles on the paradise-like Caribbean Island of Hispaniola and constitute the only nation in the world that gained its independence through a successful slave rebellion. That was in 1804.

Haiti is the poorest country in the Americas. It also happens to be the world's first postcolonial, black-led nation. Haiti's independence was inspired by the French Revolution (1789–99), which was a secularised (God-less) version of the British and American revolutions. Just as the French Revolution failed in establishing freedom and democracy, so also in two hundred years, none of Haiti's thirty-two coups, multiple dictatorships, or democratic elections, have succeeded in building political freedoms there. Lawlessness, insecurity, and instability have prevented political independence from recovering the economic possibilities witnessed even during the colonial period. Haiti has also failed to benefit from the economic potential of tourism, while the Dominican Republic, which is just on the other side of the same, beautiful island, has succeeded.

On 12 January 2010, Haiti's capital, Port-au-Prince, with a population of less than a million, was devastated by an earthquake of 7.0 magnitude. The Haitian government estimates that 316,000 people were killed immediately, and 300,000 injured. Out of the total of three million people in the country affected by the earthquake, about one million were rendered homeless. Some tens of thousands of people died after the earthquake due to lack of food, water, and medical aid.

The Disaster: Natural or Cultural?

In contrast with the Haitian earthquake that affected some 3 million people, an earthquake, also of 7.0 magnitude, struck the San Francisco Bay Area in California in the United States of America on 17 October 1989. That earthquake affected about 5 million people. But it killed only sixty-three.

Why such a difference? The Bay Area was built on a culture of relatively stronger law, justice, freedom, and consequent social trust and prosperity. In contrast, Haiti is almost totally built on a culture of corruption, oppression, social mistrust, and resultant poverty. Builders routinely disregard the rules for constructing safe buildings because political, bureaucratic, and law enforcement institutions move on the wheels of bribery.

In plain words: Haiti's earthquake was natural; its disaster is cultural.

Therefore, even though individuals needed immediate relief, the only way to rebuild Haiti is to transform its culture.

Can Hollywood's Avatar save Haiti from its corruption and spiritism?

In order to overcome its culture of corruption and poverty, Haiti needs many heroes like Jake in James Cameron's megahit movie *Avatar*. Jake was an outsider, but like Jesus Christ, he incarnated among a people who were in great need and became one of them. Like Jesus, he chose to sacrifice his own life in order to save a vulnerable people that he dearly loved.

The *Avatar's* hero—a combination of Jesus and Ram—may appear "ideal," but the film's script writer is definitely naive. The people of Haiti practice voodoo spiritism because they know better than Hollywood's romantic idealists. The Haitians know that they do not know the supreme creative spirit, whom they call *Bondey* (corruption of the French *Bon Dieu* for Good God). Since they cannot know or reach Bondey, they assume that the Creator is also incapable of reaching them, revealing Himself to them, loving them enough to discipline them or to incarnate in their midst to save them.

French Roman Catholicism tried to convert Haitian slaves in the seventeenth century; therefore, some Catholic trappings adorn Haitian voodoo. Yet, because the Haitians believe that the Creator does not care enough to interfere with human affairs, the Haitian voodoo does not fear or serve the unknown, absentee Creator.

Nevertheless, the Haitians do not think that only the material world is real. They know that spirits exist. Some of the people get possessed by spirits, and the spirits communicate with the religious leaders involved with voodoo. Devout Voodoo priests even receive certain supernatural powers from the spirits. The Haitians call these spirits Lwa or Loa, and fear and serve them. Like many of our people, and like the Na'vi people in Avatar, Haitians believe that these spirits govern nature. From disasters, such as the deadly earthquake, Haitians conclude that the spirits that govern nature or possess individuals are not always good and benevolent. The spirits may contribute to life, but they also bring disease, disasters, and death.

As Indian tantriks know well, gods and goddesses do not sacrifice themselves to save others. They demand the blood of chickens, goats, and pigs if not the blood of your neighbour or your neighbour's child before they grant your petitions. Therefore, just as many of our "holy" tantriks and ascetics become demoniacs, so the Haitians have also become like the gods and goddesses they worship—capricious, greedy, and unpredictable.

Haiti is different from the Bay Area because, in the Haitian worldview, the universe is not cosmos-ruled by the word of one Creator. They think we live in a multiverse—a chaos-governed by many unpredictable deities. This worldview does not encourage a systematic study of nature (science) or an attempt to govern and manage nature (technology). Since the universe has no Law Giver who will hold us accountable, there is no need to be a law-abiding citizen—especially if you can bribe human rulers just as your priests bribe the gods.

Could Cameron's portrayal of America be prophetic?

Cameron's *Avatar* portrays atheist (secular, unprincipled, greed-driven) America as a brutal superpower, ever ready to sacrifice simple, nature-worshipping people at the altar of economic greed.

In reality, however, earthquake-stricken Haiti, saw a very different America—a nation full of people who are quick to give up some of their own pleasures and even essential to provide billions of dollars in aid; a nation filled with churches that are sending thousands of volunteers to serve the helpless; an army that will spend its resources to rescue the trapped and save aid workers from mobs of greedy, spirit-worshipping Haitians who will loot food from the mouths even of orphans and lonely elderly people.

In spite of that, the truth is that, as atheism becomes more and more of a mask for intellectual arrogance, James Cameron's *Avatar* could turn out to be a prophetic portrayal of what America may become. Following the European Enlightenment, American intellectuals also learned what Indians and Haitians have always known: by itself—that is, without revelation—the human mind cannot know the Creator nor can it know or discover His moral law or, for that matter, His saving grace because it cannot answer the question: Does our inability to reach Him prevent Him from incarnating to save us? The Enlightenment's intellectual arrogance prevented secular Europe and America from seeking God's grace and revelation. Therefore, professing themselves to be intellectuals, they are continuing to march towards self-destructive folly:

America's godless, secular intelligentsia has succeeded in eliminating the *spirit* from the educational process. As a result, public universities are becoming factories that churn out well-informed and skilled leaders who lack moral character.

The brightest of these university graduates now control a significant section of corporate America. Their amoral, greed-driven financial management caused the economic crisis that began in 2007-2008. Honest tax payers were forced to bail out Wall Street, but the crisis continues to haunt hundreds of millions in America and around the world.

Amoral intellectual elitism is now crippling American politics. At the moment of writing, President Obama's number one domestic priority—healthcare reform—lies derailed, in shambles. The Supreme Court will finally decide whether it is even legal. "Reforming" healthcare sounds like a good thing, but if the ruling party is really doing something good, why does it have to bribe its own senators and trade unions with hundreds of millions of dollars to pass a health reform Bill?

Secular materialism, which rejects both the world of the spirit and anything to do with transcendental standards in morality, has already corrupted politics. Now it is also corrupting the American army: Open promotion of homosexuality is a reversal of a historic policy that ensured that officers do not use their power to sexually oppress their juniors; now the US authorities have told American soldiers that they do not need to fear God or live under His moral authority. Actually, greed-driven capitalists, who control so much of the American government and media, are increasing their grip over the army as well. Given this trajectory, it is certain that America will soon become worse than Saddam Hussein's Iraq, which marched its tanks into Kuwait to loot its oil wealth. When that happens, America will be what *Avatar* portrays—incomparably more dreadful than even Hitler's Germany.

Cameron may be prophetic in his portrayal of America yet, America can be saved from its encroaching corruption and destruction. It can repent and return to the spirituality that created the Bay Area's relatively just, compassionate, and law-abiding capitalism powered by scientific research and technology.

What about Haitians... and Indians?

The Bay Area that withstood the 1989 earthquake is now home to tens of thousands of Indians who lead the technological and financial sectors. Their success demonstrates that India (and Haiti) do not need to be backward. We have the intelligence to move forward. But we already know what Cameron does not know: The spirits of trees and rivers, astrology, and mythology do not save us from our sin. They enslave individuals and whole nations in fear, superstition, and corruption. We, the tree and spirit worshippers, are not Noble Savages of Hollywood's romantic idealists. We, the tree-worshipping poor peasants of India, share the same corrupt nature as the Haitians exhibit. We do need a saviour, an Avatar who is an incarnation of divine love. But such a saviour needs to be better than James Cameron's Avatar. An adequate saviour needs to sacrifice himself to save us from the demons within us, from the sin that rules our hearts, including the sin of worshipping false gods, whether of trees, or of demonic deities.

Chapter Eleven

India's Backwards
Need a Better Avatar
The Congress Working Committee Debates Maoists

Our poor do want development. But they don't want it for the super-rich; they want development to benefit their children.

You are not in Hollywood's Pandora... where James Cameron's "Avatar" incarnated as a Na'vi to save the tribals from greed-driven, brutal capitalists. You are in Mahatma Gandhi's land of non-violence, where snakes and monkeys are gods and trees and women are goddesses, and yet where paramilitary forces can slice off a 25-year-old woman's breasts before butchering her and her elderly parents and chopping off three fingers from her 2-year-old toddler. Why?

Because, her parents were alleged to be Maoist informers.

If so, why not present the case against them before a court? Aren't we a democracy, ruled by law?

Of course! We are the world's largest democracy, but who fights a war with democratic niceties?

What?... Is India at war?

Mother India today

Why else would anyone blast a bus carrying twelve Special Officers twenty feet up in the air with sophisticated explosives? Does that sound like a law-and-order problem to you? Don't you know that enemy nations have already trained and equipped a standing army of ten thousand insurgents to become brutal beasts? According to reports, at least another lakh of trained rebels are living within our borders as "normal" people. Justice is for humans, not animals. The bus had twice as many civilians as paramilitary officers. Had these heartless terrorists allowed civilians to get off the bus before blowing it up, we could have treated them with civilised justice. The Prime Minister knows what he is talking about when he says that these Hindus-turned-Maoists are a much greater internal security threat to our nation than the few Muslims turned Jihadists.

Wait a minute! Why were these Special Officers going to war in a bus filled with civilians? Do our forces lack vehicles? And is our intelligence so incompetent that no one warned them of a possible ambush? Did they forget that just weeks earlier an army of a thousand guerrillas had almost eliminated a whole unit of Special Forces in that very same district?

***

"Our intelligence is as competent as any in the world," one can virtually hear the bespectacled home minister arguing before his colleagues in the Congress Working Committee. "We expected the ambush; that's precisely why we sent them in plain clothes in a public bus, rather than in a Special Forces' vehicle. An army truck would have drawn attention. We *have* learned our lesson; that's why these brave officers were trying to save their lives [using civilians as human shields]. We wouldn't have lost these lives if you had listened to me in the first place. I sought your permission to send them in an Air Force helicopter, but you wouldn't approve. First you tie my hands; then you blame our intelligence as incompetent!

"Make no mistake! Everyone knows that our forces can finish off these bloody brutes in days. But the nation is wondering whether our party has what it takes to meet our enemies' challenge, protect innocent civilians, and harness our nation's natural resources. Meanwhile, the BJP strikes a chord in our national pride when it argues that India can become a superpower, but the Congress party lacks the political will to make India the world's greatest economy. A ragtag band of ruthless rebels is holding up the development of our tribal areas, but we are so concerned about the Western idea of "human rights" that we would not even acknowledge that we are at war. Why keep a standing army if we can't use it to defend national interests from these foreign-trained militants? "How long will we hide our heads in the sand? The world already knows that these backward Bahujans are being used by our enemies to wage a war against India's economic future. Our industrial houses are anxious to pour billions of dollars into building mega projects to generate electricity, make steel, mine coal, bauxite, and what not. China is beating us at almost every turn because it has given up Maoism in favour of capitalism. And yet we are allowing China's outdated Maoism to frustrate those willing to invest in our development. The lesson we need to learn from Ma and China is ruthlessness in governing.

"State governments have signed any number of Memorandum of Understandings with world-renowned industrialists. [And remember the donations we took from them to capture power!] We are honour bound to deliver under-utilised lands to these builders of India's future. Let's face it: investment dollars aren't going to wait forever. Available capital is finite, and it will go where governments are progressive enough to support development with all their might. If we fail to honour our promises, industrialists will back a party that has the guts to support progress.

"Besides, our universities are churning out some of the world's best-trained graduates. This young talent isn't going to wait either. Our graduates will grab the first opportunity to use their training. They will build other nations, as our best brains migrate. The maximum damage these Marxist avatars will do is to the tribals themselves: if they don't get them killed, they will condemn them to perpetual backwardness."

The Gandhi Avatar

(*As this fictitious meeting listens to his monologue*) The home minister perhaps looks to the elderly chairman with a turban and grave looks to see what he thinks: Are Maoists the saviours of poor tribals, or are they our greatest internal security threat? Would the chairman take a stand, or would he be bullied into inaction by the anti-development *Outlook* of Leftist avatars? But the chairman's eyes turn to the only woman in the room... so every head in CWC turns towards her.

The woman turns to her son to see if he still thinks that his future is tied to his mother's.

The son is wise. "Look! If my mother's name was Indira Gandhi, I would be Sanjay. I would then spearhead this battle, not the home minister. But Mummy didn't choose the kursi (chair) she had. She knows our obligations to the industrial houses, but she also knows that ultimately, she owes her position not to them but to Destiny. Our nation's destiny is tied to her, and her destiny forces her to ask: What would Mahatma Gandhi do?

"We know that the Mahatma would go on a fast unto death against our government's brutality as much as against Maoist violence. Tribal "Gandhis-with-guns' have no regard for the Mahatma's legacy, but we have to at least pay lip-service.

"The problem that the Mahatma doesn't solve is how to persuade backward Bahujans to give up their lands for developing mega industries. In fact, the Mahatma's answer is embarrassing: He would fast in Birla Mansion, teaching Tatas and Ambanis to spin their own khadi, milk their own goats, and forget industrialization. He would have condemned us to the stone-age. It was the foresight of our first prime minister that saved our country from the Mahatma's idealistic nonsense. Thanks to Pandit Nehru, now even the Vedanta company wants to borrow financial 68 and intellectual capital from the Church of England to chase the maya of mega-industries. Our Swadeshi party is also backing Western capitalist Vedanta.

"Mummy's *Inconvenient Truth* is that Hollywood's filthy-rich Green avatars are bullying us to follow the Mahatma. Nobel Laureates like Al Gore do not want us to use coal to generate cheap power. They will honour our culture if we sit naked and meditate on our mountains of coals in pristine jungles, eat wild berries, and learn how to worship trees from their 3-D movies, using their solar batteries and windmills.

"The silver lining is that Marxists have delivered our tribals from the opium of Hollywood's hypocritical spirituality. Our poor do want development. But they don't want it for the super-rich; they want development to benefit their children. So, the question is how to ensure that our national development will benefit the backwards and not send them to live in slums."

"The answer," the woman spoke up, "is obvious: The Congress has the political will, what our nation lacks is cultural will."" The originality of her observation made the committee curious; so, she continued, "It's time we come to terms with what our reformers, such as Jotiba Phule, were trying to tell us 150 years ago. Our Five-Year Plans built schools in these backward areas, but our attempts have failed. Last year, all the teachers fled from their posts in one of these Maoist-occupied territories. Parents didn't protect the teachers because what these well-paid public teachers taught did not equip their children to benefit from our mega projects. Those teachers are still drawing salaries, but they live in their homes and use their work time to make additional money offering private tuition to the children of our netas (petty politicians) and bureaucrats.

"What do you think is happening to the village children? In one case, the Maoists invited South Indian missionaries to give English education to these children. The missionaries sought permission from the district collector. With the chief minister's consent, these missionaries are using empty government schools to educate children. At times the Maoists use the same government buildings to train older kids to fight against the state.

"Why don't we send Saraswati Shishu Mandirs to run these schools?" A CWC member inquired.

A former chief minister of a central Indian state musters up the courage to answer, "It's time that our nation comes to terms with really inconvenient truths. It's been more than six decades since we assumed the responsibility to govern our nation. History gave us enough time to develop the tribals of the Red Corridor to become like the tribals of Mizoram, who take care of their own development and offer exemplary service to the nation in all walks of life. Why did independent India lose sixty years and make this bloody mess? It is primarily because we allowed militant Hindus to use the Niyogi Commission to drive out the missionaries who were educating the Bahujans at great personal sacrifice.

"Our party collaborated with Hindutva, hoping to woo Hindu voters. Congress governments encouraged Hindu missionaries to move into the vacuum and convert tribals to Hinduism. Has that strategy helped? It was doomed to fail because no Brahmin priest, however good his intentions, can turn a Shudra or an Adivasi into a Brahmin. The best that the tribal converts to Hinduism have done is to team up with greedy netas and corrupt bureaucrats to start Salwa Judum. It is funded by the state and the capitalists, and it started the current vicious cycle of ugly violence that has grown into this magic war.

Many tribals trust Maoists more than they trust Hindu missionaries. Historians will contend that the explosive that blew up that bus was not foreign but swadeshi: it was made by fusing Hinduism with capitalism. The caste system that has oppressed the Bahujan for millennia is being reinforced by democratic capitalism. This mixture is proving to be deadly. It has turned our beautiful cities, such as Mumbai, into slums that *Slumdog Millionaire* showed to the whole world. Hindu-capitalism is the root of this war."

No one had expected this (imaginary) Congress Working Committee session to go this way. So, once again, they turned to the chairman for directions. The confidentiality of the meeting allowed him to surprise everyone: "Let me be frank," the chairman admitted, "the chief minister did not allow Christian missionaries from South India to use state schools without consulting me. I consented because the Bahujan are beginning to agree with Mahatma Phule. Politics has failed, Hindu missions have failed. It was the decision to ban foreign missionaries that created the vacuum being filled by Maoists. Therefore, the Bahujan are beginning to agree with Mahatma Phule that Baliraja (Jesus Christ) may be the only avatar who can save the backward from this horrible war between Hindu, Maoist, Leftist, and Capitalist saviours. Tribals can benefit from industrialization if they are educated. But government schools have already failed. So, the parents want missionaries to come back. Fortunately, Jesus is inspiring tens of thousands of Indians to go to remote areas to serve. The Maoists respect them because they themselves cannot do what the missionaries do. Therefore, in the interest of education and development, I agreed with the chief minister that a Christ-inspired mission may be the force that could win the battle against Maoist militancy."

PART IV

ESCAPE ROUTES

Chapter Twelve
Our Budgets and Our Backwardness

Our rulers must stop coveting the wealth that we create, and we must stop stealing the taxes that are needed to pay for our nation's welfare.

Those who read newspapers probably know that if Parliament votes against the budget, the prime minister and his government have to resign. Why? Because, the rulers cannot collect one paisa from us as tax or spend our tax money without our approval. We elect Members of Parliament to scrutinise and approve a budget on our behalf because we trust them to understand and represent our interest, the interest of the backward Bahujan (majority).

Why then are we so poor? The history of our taxation gives one important explanation. Angus Maddison's massive study, "The World Economy: A Millennial Perspective," published by the Center for Economic Co-operation and Development, estimates that in the year 1800, after Great Britain had colonised a great part of the world, including India, the total revenue it collected from the whole world was £16 million (Rs 179 crores at today's rates). In contrast, two hundred years prior to that, in the year 1600 (that is, the year in which the British East India Company was formed), Mughal Emperor Akbar collected £17.5 million (Rs. 196 crores) within India from our impoverished forefathers! And Akbar was the best of the Mughal rulers. He did use some of that money to give us unity, law and a relatively "just" government. Because his rule rested on the sword, Akbar had no need to ask us how much he could tax us, or how he should spend our tax money.

Akbar's son Jehangir was too debauched with power and too

drunk on wine and opium to have the time to govern. Obsession with grandeur so blinded Akbar's grandson, Shah Jahan, that he could not even see our backwardness. Because of his projects such as the Taj Mahal, the Peacock Throne, and the Red Fort, it was said, "The world had run out of gold." Soon after Shah Jahan began building the Taj Mahal, British merchant Peter Mundy travelled from Surat to Agra to get his permission for the British to trade in India. This is how Mundy described his journey in 1631:

> "From Surat to this place, all the highway was stowed with dead people, our noses never free from the stink of them.. .women were seen to roast their children... a man or a woman no sooner dead, but they were cut in pieces to be eaten."

Why? The monsoon had failed, and people had nothing to eat. But this wasn't the first time that Indra—our god of rain—had let his worshippers down. Why weren't warehouses made to store grain? After all, the warehousing technology invented in Egypt under the wise rule of the Hebrew prime minister, Joseph, was known in India at least since the Indus Valley Civilization. Lack of knowledge was not the problem. The trouble was with taxation. If the ruler is going to take away your surplus produce to build a monument for the bones of his beloved wife, then where is the incentive to develop your land, produce extra, and save some for a rainless day?

If foreign (Mughal) rulers were like that, were our own Hindu rulers more just and compassionate? I was born in Chhatarpur but grew up in Allahabad and Indore. In 1976 my wife and I decided to go back to Chhatarpur district to serve my people who had remained in the powerful bonds of backwardness for thousands of years. We lived about twenty kilometres from Khajuraho. Every day plane loads of tourists came to the Khajuraho temples to see the sculptures of our naked priests and rulers embracing Devadasis in sexual ecstasy. These temples were built by our devout religious philosophers and architects a thousand years ago. Few tourists ever ventured out into neighbouring villages to see our neighbours barely able to feed themselves or clothe their bodies. Our neighbours were still living in mud huts with thatched roofs, just like our forefathers a thousand years ago. They knew how to build those stone temples, but they were not allowed to build homes for their children.

Those erotic tantric temples have survived because the Muslim invaders did not get as far as conquering that area. These temples, therefore, are a testimony to the fact that our Hindu rulers did not care for our people any more than the Muslims who followed them. My people lived in mud huts because our Hindu rulers taxed their wealth away to finance their royal and religious decadence.

According to some accounts, the Mauryas are considered more benevolent kings. Particularly under the Emperor Ashoka (a convert to Buddhism), farmers were freed of tax and crop collection burdens that had been imposed by (earlier) regional kings. A national system of taxation was introduced, which was fair but strict. This was also advised by the pragmatic principles of Kautilya's *Arthashastra (economics)* as a way to earn the loyalty of subjects. However, if this benevolence is historical fact, it was based on pragmatism, not on principles derived from our philosophies or rooted in our culture.

The present system that requires rulers to obtain our permission to collect and spend our taxes is a precious gift of the hated British Raj. Lord Macaulay, the British historian who knew India as well as anyone else in the nineteenth century, acknowledged that the British East India Company began its rule in Bengal as a "gang of public robbers." Hindu aristocracy hates Macaulay because he played a decisive role in turning this "rule of an evil genie" into a just government. Macaulay grew up in the company of great Bible-believing British MPs such as William Wilberforce and Charles Grant. These leaders started a sustained campaign to give India a better government than the British themselves had. They were driven by the commands of their Lord Jesus that his followers should love their neighbours and even their enemies as much as they loved themselves.

Why didn't the British continue looting us to build a better Khajuraho or Taj Mahal in London? The Bible tells us that King Solomon built a magnificent temple for God with generous contributions from people. Then Solomon went on to put on his people an unbearable economic burden to build palaces for his wives and temples for their idols. When Rehoboam, his son, succeeded him on the throne, people's representatives requested him to ease this tax burden. He consulted the Jewish Elders, who knew that "You shall not steal" and "You shall not covet your neighbour's property" were God's commands. Therefore, these God-given laws were as binding on rulers as on the common man. Therefore, the elders advised the king to serve the people so that they may in turn serve him willingly. The King's younger friends, however, wanted power. So, in total disregard for God's law as well as for wise counsel, they recommended that the king become tougher than his father. Rehoboam listened to his power-hungry friends and decided to increase the tax even more. The people revolted, and the kingdom split into Judah and Israel. Both became too weak to withstand the aggression of Iraq (Assyria and Babylon). The Jews became slaves: first to their own exploitative kings and later to invaders.

The nations that derived their political theory from biblical history became different from the rest of the world. They became relatively just, free, and prosperous. During the English Civil War (1642-1651), John Hampden stated this biblical principle in the famous statement, "What an English king has no right to demand, an English subject has a right to refuse." The American Revolution expressed the same principle in the slogan, "No taxation without representation."

Charles Grant and William Pitt made just taxation in India a British ideal. Independent India is blessed because the writers of our Constitution, such as Dr. Ambedkar, decided to institutionalise this biblical political wisdom. This biblical view of taxation is the primary factor behind the rise of the middle class. For the first time in our history, it has become possible for the common man to enjoy the wealth he creates. Yet, this wise theory has not been able to end our backwardness because it is only a derivative theory. We are yet to internalise the source of that theory—the Bible—that can transform our individual and cultural soul. Allow me to explain.

A million-dollar question

Will backwardness end if the budget is prepared and managed by "Backward" politicians?

It is evident to all that our so-called lower-caste politicians are just as capable of wasting our tax money as the Mughals. Our leaders also build monuments for their prestige and for preserving the memories of their dead. They can be just as foolish as was King Rehoboam disregarding time-tested wisdom in favour of the advice, this time of socialist companions who want to promote big, inefficient, wasteful state-controlled projects as symbols of their power that also provide juicy opportunities for syphoning off wealth by corrupt means into your own pocket and/ or the pockets of your relatives and supporters.

American businesses are supposed to represent "greedy" capitalism, India is a poor and "spiritual" country, but in proportionate terms, the black economy is vastly greater than America's.

The Black economy makes it necessary to extract more taxes from those people who cannot hide their income. That makes taxation appear as a government's wish to covet and steal our money. In response, unless people obey some compulsion of conscience, it is easy for people to be tempted into devising ingenious ways of evading taxes. Respected social scientists, such as Arun Kumar, estimated that in the mid-1950s, our black economy accounted for only 3 percent of the national economy. By 1995, it had become 40 percent—that is, about $1 trillion—that was, more than the industrial and agricultural sectors combined. Clearly, in such a situation, the political theories behind the English and American revolutions are no help. Now, in 2024, based on CBI investigations, Wikipedia estimates that the black money may amount to ₹28 lakh crores, or approximately US $3.33 trillion.

The corruption of our economy represents the corruption of our souls. The Lord Jesus said that we had to be born again by the Spirit of God in order to see the kingdom of God—that is, to enjoy the rule of God's just law and peace and prosperity that result from God's rule—in this life and into eternity. We need the Holy Spirit of God to write the law of God in our hearts, so that our rulers will stop coveting the wealth that we create, and so that we will stop coveting and stealing the taxes that we need to pay for our nation's welfare.

Chapter Thirteen
The Maoist War Against Robber Capitalism

The most liberated and developed tribes in India are in the North-East. They followed Jesus, not Chairman Mao.

On Saturday, 12 June 2010 at 10 a.m., army-trained and backed Special Forces launched massive Operation Hawk to capture a hilltop on the Jharkhand-Orissa border that had become a Maoist camp. After more than sixteen hours of gun grenade and mortar battle, at 4 p.m. on Sunday, 13 June, India Inc. declared victory, claiming that three hundred Maoists had fled the camp. Indian forces airlifted the wounded on "our" side for medical help, admitting one casualty and asserting —without any evidence—that Maoists must have carried their dead on their backs. No photographs were produced, and no dead bodies were found.

Four days later, in a different operation in West Bengal, heroes of our Special Forces returned from a triumphant hunt of Maoists, parading the dead body of one Indian young woman carried like a wild pig on a pole.

The army has declared its resolve not to get involved directly—at least not for now. To begin with, Sonia Gandhi has learned from the pain of widowhood. She seems to understand that it was not a woman Tamilian suicide-bomber but the arrogance of power that killed her husband. In using the Indian army to save Sri Lanka from Tamil Tigers, he lost his own life. The Tamil Tigers also humbled the Indian army enough for our generals to understand that no army can win a war against the poor. To fight 100,000 Maoists moving freely in hilly terrain extending more than a thousand miles, the army will have to deploy at least 500,000 men. In response, the Maoists will need to do nothing except shoot down an occasional helicopter or army jeep, and move into towns with their relatives, living like normal people, until the army is sent back to the barracks elsewhere in the country. Meanwhile, our heroic soldiers will harass, kill, and rape innocent civilians—providing horror stories, captured by CNN-IBN and other reporters for audiences all over the world.

The many-sided cost of army action is actually astronomical. Isn't it easier for our ruling elite to ask their capitalist buddies (who know how to buy parliamentarians not only in India but even in America) to bribe and buy off Maoist leaders and make them MLAs, MPs, and ministers? Maoist leaders may well consider such offers if cameras capture enough of their comrades being carried about like dead pigs. But it needs no great imagination or intelligence to understand that such solutions work only until the next election. Committed Maoists will label their "for-sale" leaders as betrayers and fill the leadership positions that are vacated with more committed revolutionaries.

The Case Against Robber Capitalism

During the 2011 general election, Mr. L. K. Advani promised that if the nation voted to make him the prime minister, he would bring back to India $1.4 trillion in black money hoarded abroad. Baba Ramdev has now made that his political platform. The facts suggest that India's Hindu capitalism, America's secular capitalism, and Christian capitalism are entirely different socio-economic systems. By *Hindu Capitalism*, I mean a "free market" system that worships Lakshmi (the goddess of wealth) and derives its ethical values from its pursuit of wealth. It is an economic system not controlled by a Holy God who commands, "Thou shalt not covet," or steal or kill. The term Hindu Capitalism does not imply that every Hindu businessman is a lawbreaker or that Muslims, Christians, or Buddhists do not practice Robber or Criminal Capitalism. The term is meant to describe our current economic system produced by India's Hindu ethos that rejects the biblical idea that God is holy and his moral law is binding on all spheres of our lives, including the way we make and spend money.

From where did our Hindu capitalists get their "dirty money"? One source of it is illegal mining. In the Indian states where Operation Hawk took place, it is reported that 60 percent of all mines may be illegal. Maoists are fighting robber capitalists who have been plundering the nation's mineral wealth for as many as twenty years without even applying for a license. Some miners, who did file the required applications, did not bother obtaining licenses because legal mining and banking require one to keep proper accounts, get them audited, and pay taxes. If capitalists do that, they cannot also finance corrupted democracy or maintain private militia ("security"). In order to mine, one has to keep politicians and bureaucrats in one's pocket (and harem).

The Maoist case against Hindu Capitalism is simple: A significant section of our industrialists, politicians, their (un)holy gods, gurus, and godmen, as well as their best-educated, secular, Gazette administrative and police officers, have joined hands to become criminal mafias backed by official militias called "Special Forces" that, with unofficial militias such as Salwa Judum, started the round of tragic violence.

But hasn't the government spent thousands of crores of rupees to educate and equip these backward STs, SCs, and OBCs and the leftist leaders? Why can't they participate in our free-market economy and benefit from it?

Consider also that, while Indian capitalists hide their wealth abroad, British taxpayers have donated 340 million pounds to educate India's poor through the Education for All programme called *Sarva Shiksha Abhiyan*. Much of this money has either vanished or has been misused. The Auditor General of India admitted that at least 14 million pounds have been used to buy things like air-conditioners for village schools that have neither buildings nor electricity. British tax-payers are already burdened with the responsibility to save Greece, Spain, Italy, Portugal, etc. Therefore, they are agitated at our immorality that loves Lakshmi, not the poor for whom the money is donated. In order to appease his tax-payers, Andrew Mitchel, the British Secretary of State for International Development, has promised to institutionalise zero tolerance for (at least) Indian abuse of British generosity.

But Why Can't Indian Maoists Follow Chinese "Marxism"?

China's Marxist Capitalism is doing better than India's Hindu Capitalism. Nevertheless, Marxism's fundamental problem is that it is a corruption of the Bible's worldview. Moses, the Jewish liberator and lawgiver, began writing the Bible after God sent him to Egypt to liberate the Hebrews from nearly four centuries of slavery. Had Karl Marx been steeped in Hindu/Buddhist worldview, he would have deemed slavery to be a result of their karma. Were he a Muslim, he would have accepted slavery of the toiling masses as Allah's will. He happened to have been a Christian of Jewish descent, living in Christian England. Therefore, he had a biblical bias in favour of the poor. Marx's optimism that slaves can possess "a land flowing with milk and honey" also came from the Bible; only in the Bible does the Creator-Saviour God reveal Himself as one who is against dehumanising socio-economic and political slavery. That is why the Jews looked forward to a divine Messiah who would be a Liberator.

When Jesus was born, the Jews had been looking for their promised Messiah. They assumed that he would be a God-sent Maoist-type guerrilla leader, who would fight the Romans (the oppressors). The Jewish masses came to Jesus to find healing and food, and to learn about the Kingdom of God, but they could not believe that someone who carried his cross (instead of a sword) could save them from the tyranny of the Roman military. Yet, the fact is that ultimately, Jesus conquered Rome. As in Rome, and later in the whole of Europe, there is only one hope for India's Backward: a pro-poor Messiah, a Good Shepherd who lays down his life for the sheep.

The most liberated and developed tribes in India are in the North-East. They followed Jesus, not Chairman Mao. Maoism has won over the tribals in Chhattisgarh, Jharkhand, and Orissa only because militant Hindus and the Congress party joined hands in using the Niyogi Commission report to chase away Christian missions that were developing their tribal communities. Without a Saviour who teaches India to seek not Lakshmi but the Kingdom of God, our economic development could become our doom. Our mega mining and industrial projects will drive the downtrodden into urban slums. If our "educated" elite who love clean cities then bulldoze their stinking slum-dwellings, where will our poor go?

Indian Army must prepare itself to save our cities

During my recent trip to India, on 7 June 2010, a senior scientist working in a multinational pharmaceutical company and his wife—a medical doctor—took me out for dinner to a newly opened restaurant in Gurgaon, on the outskirts of New Delhi. As I enjoyed the fruits of the rapidly growing Indian economy, I asked my hostess if the prosperity that I saw all around me was trickling down to the villages. Five years earlier, she had returned from Japan and America to serve the poor in fifteen villages barely thirty kilometres from Delhi's international airport. She told me that the prosperity of Delhi and Gurgaon is not reaching even ten kilometres from where we were eating.

So, how are the poor managing?

"Something strange is happening in my villages," she said. "What?" I asked.

"Five of the villages are predominantly Muslim. They were the poorest until six months ago when their men disappeared and their economy began to improve."

"Where have the men gone?"

"To Pakistan—their wives are telling me. Five years ago, there were Muslims only nominally. But now they have become staunch Muslims because a maulvi has been coming from Lucknow to teach them. He has helped the men find work in Pakistan."

"Are these men skilled or educated?"

"No, they can barely read."

"Well," I said, "illiterate Muslims going to Saudi Arabia or Dubai to work as labourers makes sense. But they may need to learn Arabic to work there. How can Pakistan's weak economy enable Indian labourers to earn enough money to send home?" "I don't know," said the good doctor. "I am telling you only what the village women have been confiding in me."

"I pray," I responded, "that these men would not return to Delhi with the kinds of resources the Maoists have acquired."

Should the army get ready to tackle the response of poor Muslims to Hindu capitalism?

The lady doctor said, "This is not an Islamic issue alone. Five years ago, even the Hindus were only nominally Hindus. But now they are having a lot of jagrans (whole-night religious singing). Most poor people are being radicalised whether by Islam, Hindutva, or Maoist guerrillas.

The Government of India has acted wisely in not sending the military against the Maoists. For the military may soon be needed to defend our metropolises from the downtrodden who are finally rising up against India's corrupt capitalism.

Chapter Fourteen
Twitter Attacking Tanks?
Muslims Meet Modernity

Can the brave and intelligent people of Libya or Iran or Saudi Arabia or Syria find inner intellectual and spiritual resources to free themselves from their traditional slavery?

In a bold statement to a world in turmoil, the American space agency, NASA, has named one of its spaceships to Mars, Zahran, after 23-year-old beautiful Sally Zahran, who was beaten to death by the security forces of Egypt's ousted dictator, Hosni Mubarak. Zahran, a university graduate in English and a translator, was one of hundreds of Egyptians willing to pay the ultimate price to throw off a 30-year-old reign of *oppression*. Now the beneficiaries of her martyrdom face the even greater challenge of establishing a just and free government that is responsive to the needs of the Egyptian people.

About 6,700-11,000 Muslims died at the hands of fellow Muslims between 18 December 2010 and 11 March 2011 in an effort to modernise a cradle of human civilization. They deserve our support and prayers that their sacrifice will help deliver their nation from a mediaeval mindset that for centuries kept much of the world, including India, in slavery.

It was the 26-year-old street vendor, Mohamed Bouazizi, in a small town in Tunisia, who lit up the spark that began this wildfire for freedom. When he was only three years old, Bouazizi lost his father, who died of a heart attack. His mother married his uncle, who became sick and was unable to support the family of six children. Bouazizi had to start working when he was ten, and by the time he was eighteen, he had to give up his own ambition for an education in order to support his mother, uncle, and sisters, one of whom he sent to study in university.

In a country with over 30 percent unemployment, Bouazizi had few options. Every application he submitted for a job was rejected. He borrowed money to buy and sell produce on the streets. His hard work made it possible for him to dream of buying a pickup truck— provided he could save something from the policemen who regularly extracted bribes from toilers like him, though they were already paid by the state to protect him and his property; some of them even worshipped in the same mosque that he did.

What he could not accept was the humiliation that was (allegedly) meted out to him by a 45- year-old city woman official, Ms. Faida Hamdi, on 17 December 2010. The previous night he had borrowed $200 to buy the produce before dawn. By 8 a.m., he was selling it on the streets.

She came along with her entourage at around 10.30 seeking a bribe. He had not had the time to earn enough to repay even the interest on his loan, but she wanted her cut first. It is said that she slapped him in the face, spat at him, confiscated his electronic weighing scales, and tossed aside his produce cart. The self-respecting young man found it hard to accept this public humiliation by a callous, arrogant, female robber! Bouazizi marched to the governor's office to complain, but he may have been too naive to realise that Ms. Hamdi was simply a part of a giant machine, a channel her superiors may have been using to syphon off the wealth created by working people. When the governor refused to see him, Bouazizi doused himself with some flammable liquid, and in less than an hour after his humiliation, he was aflame in front of a local government building. His self-immolation sparked the deadly demonstrations and riots throughout Tunisia that forced then-president Zine El Abidine Ben Ali to step down on January 14, 2011. He had ruled his country for twenty-three years, bringing it to ruin.

Unemployment and underemployment give young people time to explore social media such as Facebook and Twitter. It was such unregulated media, rather than the established press, university, or political forums that turned the spectacular success of the Tunisian protest into a wildfire. It was social media that brought young people like Sally Zahran to Tahrir (liberty) Square in Cairo, Egypt. Abdel Moneim Jafar, a 49-year-old restaurant owner, demonstrated that they were not out to shout shallow slogans. He followed Bouazizi's example, by setting himself alight in front of the Egyptian Parliament. Such desperate acts forced the resignation of Egypt's president, Hosni Mubarak, on 11 February 2011. During 30 years of his rule, his family is estimated to have amassed $80 billion at his people's expense!

This liberation from corrupt dictatorships in Tunisia and Egypt fuelled the fires of freedom in Yemen, Jordan, Morocco, Bahrain, Saudi Arabia, Algeria, Iraq, Iran, and Libya. It is in Libya and Syria that Islam finally confronted the challenge of modernity. When it became clear that Islamic authoritarianism would suppress democracy in Libya, Europe's need for cheap oil inspired NATO's "humanitarian bombs" in support of the rebels.

Gaddafi's regime, like most Islamic regimes, had been known for silencing legitimate questions, oppressing rival tribes, sponsoring terrorism during the 1970s and 1980s, assassinating expatriate opposition leaders, and organising the system on the basis of crass nepotism. Through control over the nation's oil, his family had amassed a fortune of at least $70 billion. A part of this loot was used to buy the loyalty of his tribe as well as foreign mercenaries who kept Gaddafi's gang in power for 41 years. His militia was well funded to fight for years and crush its opponents.

In spite of his status as an outrageous rogue, initially the West decided not to defend the people of Libya without support from other neighbouring nations. It stepped into the combat zone after it became apparent that the corrupt and oppressive heads of other oil rich Muslim nations would prefer to follow the Middle-Eastern way represented by Gaddafi's brutal tactics rather than the aberration that happened in Tunisia and Egypt, where leaders, even though they were corrupt, eventually did, resign. Since Twitter cannot fight tanks bought by Allah-given oil, the real question is: Where can the brave and intelligent people of Libya, Iran, Saudi Arabia, or Syria find the intellectual and spiritual resources to free themselves from their traditional slavery?

Gaddafi saw himself not as a dictator, but as the father of one of the wealthiest nations in the whole of Africa. So, why did he send tanks to butcher his own "children"? On 22 February 2011, the "Father of Libya" explained on national television that he saw the protesters as nothing more than "rats and cockroaches." That shocked the world. Had he, however, described all human beings as qualitatively no different than amoebas and cockroaches, then every secular university in the West would have endorsed his philosophy. Virtually every liberal who chooses to abort a baby agrees with Gaddafi that, intrinsically, a human being is no more valuable than a rat. If the value of a human being is only what is given to her or him by a society, what is wrong if Muslim nations choose not to ascribe human dignity or inalienable rights to non-Muslims or even fellow Muslims from other tribes or sects?

Modern tools such as Twitter and Facebook played a great role in weeding out dictators from Tunisia and Egypt. But weeding is only a minor step in good gardening. The Bouazizis and Zahrans, who want to build new nations, have to find inner strength to question the fundamental philosophical assumptions of their societies. They cannot afford to be deceived by America's Declaration of Independence, which suggests that human dignity, equality, and rights are "self-evident" truths. Human beings do have unique dignity and fundamental rights endowed by their Creator. But that is known through God's revelation in the Bible. The idea that they are "self-evident" is a myth invented in Scotland and promoted by the American Enlightenment.

Human dignity, equality, and rights have never been self-evident to any society outside Europe and North America, except as a result of the influence of those societies. Nor did the architect of America's Declaration of Independence, Thomas Jefferson, believe that these truths were self-evident to human beings. That is why in the original draft of the Declaration he wrote, "We hold these truths to be sacred and undeniable." By "sacred," he meant revealed by God in the Bible. He changed the words under pressure from deists who, having pirated the idea of human dignity from the Bible, tried to make it dependent on human common sense.

As for us in India, we are "backward" because human equality was never self-evident to any Hindu sage. What is self-evident is that human beings are unequal. That is why Hindu philosophers thought that the Creator must have created us unequal and our karma must have aggravated our intrinsic inequality. Just as blindness to the reality of human dignity lies at the heart of Hinduism, so does rejection of it constitute the very rationale for Islam's existence.

Islam was born in a rejection of the historical source of the modern belief in human dignity. Islam denies that human beings are so precious to God that He came to this earth and died on the cross for our salvation. Christ's sacrifice is far more profound than the martyrdoms of Bouazizi and Sally Zahran. Islam insists that God is so majestic that he cannot possibly become human and die as a sacrificial victim.

Islam's denial of the Cross has had far-reaching cultural implications for Muslim societies. It has prevented the development of a culture where the devout will sacrifice themselves to serve others. Instead, it keeps breeding not just dictators like Saddam Hussain and Gaddafi but also devout suicide bombers to treat human beings like rats and cockroaches. The Bible viewed human beings as special; created in God's own image. The Bible's view of unique human dignity was articulated in Europe during the fourteenth and fifteenth centuries, when the pioneers of the European Renaissance took Islam's intellectual challenge seriously. As I have discussed in *The Book That Made Your World: How the Bible Created the Soul of Western Civilization*, it was on the basis of God's revelation in the Bible, that writers like Petrarch Salutati, Lorenzo Valla, and Pico Della Mirandola concluded that human beings are creatures just as rats and cockroaches are creatures. What makes us unique and valuable is that the Creator made us (male and female) in His own image to manage this earth as His stewards. These writers agreed with Islam that God could not become a dog. However, if humans are made in His image, then God could become a human. But did He?

Muslim intellectuals insisted that it was "illogical" to think that God could become a helpless little baby and die as a powerless victim on the cross. What these intellectuals did not realise was that this faith in "logic" came not from divine revelation but from Aristotle, and it prevented Islamic culture from developing modern science. Europe birthed modern science because scholars such as William of Ockham at Oxford and Jean Buridan at Paris were able to liberate Europe from bondage to Aristotelian logic. As they studied the Bible, they realised that God existed before the cosmos. He is not a part of the universe. Therefore, He is free—not bound by the logic that exists in the universe only because of His free choices.

This insight into the metaphysical freedom of God implied that the Greeks were wrong in assuming that truth could be deduced logically. Because God is free, we need to go out to observe what God has actually done. Logic has to be subservient to empirical observation. Logical conclusions have to be subject to the authority of observed facts. In other words, the question is not whether or not God could or can become human, but whether or not He actually did. And what if He did actually become a human and die for us? That would imply that human beings are precious. Every human being is valuable, not because society says so, but because the Creator holds him precious—an object of his unique love.

This idea of the freedom of God had a second profound practical implication. If human beings are made in God's image... if we are made to be creative and develop our own culture on this earth... then it must be that the state exists to protect the freedom that God has given to human beings. Our freedom is not a ruler's gift to us. Rather, authority is delegated to a ruler so that he or she may protect our God-given liberties.

Islam denies freedom to Muslims because it denies freedom to

God. It denies God the freedom to love us enough to come to this earth to save us. Since Islam does not permit God to come to his earth to establish his kingdom, Muslims have no option but to be ruled exclusively by flawed and corrupt human rulers. Islam ruled over much of India for almost eight centuries. However, during that time it did not produce a single Phule, Gandhi, Ambedkar, or Nehru. Neither Islam nor Hinduism cultivated freedom, because human dignity and liberty are not aspects of their worldviews.

In the sixteenth century, the printing press helped liberate Europe by making it possible for Europeans to debate the validity of ideas that sustained oppressive socio-political structures. Yet it was not printing that reformed Europe, for printing had existed in China for five hundred years before Guttenberg invented his press in 1450. Europe's Reformation began only when the Christian "Protestant" reformers like Martin Luther and John Calvin began using the press. Likewise, today's social media can enable brave young Arab and North African "protestants" to reform their nations, provided they are willing to debate beliefs held by tyrants such as Muammar Gaddafi. The question is: Will Islam tolerate such freedom to seek truth and also to communicate a passion for seeking and finding truth?

PART V

MIGHTY WARRIORS

Chapter Fifteen
Can Yoga Cure Corruption?

Corruption is a moral issue and none of the philosophies that promote yoga diagnose human problem in moral terms.

Raja Ram Mohan Roy, Keshab Chandra Sen and Mahatma Jotirao Phule... knew Western missionaries intimately. They could see how their personal lives, even though imperfect, differed so radically from our "saints", as well as from greedy, arrogant Europeans.

In 2011, Social activist Anna Hazare and (now discredited) yoga guru Baba Ramdev focused the world's attention on our national disease: corruption. For over 3,000 years, Hinduism deprived the Shudras of opportunities that come from knowledge, governance, and finance. Now, education, democracy, and free-market economics have begun to undo those fetters. Yet corruption continues to barricade our people into backwardness. It prevents the poor from developing their God-given potential and using it for the common good. Baba Ramdev was right in insisting that those (mainly) educated, upper-caste Hindus who have looted the nation and hidden their black money abroad are anti-national. If that capital was available, our hard-working entrepreneurs could create jobs for perhaps tens of millions of unemployed people. Corruption keeps us backward. But why are we Indians so corrupt?

Baba Ramdev and Anna Hazare have demonstrated but not conceded (yet) that the corruption of our souls is a disease that neither yoga nor civil society can cure. If the Baba were to campaign against black money within India, he would probably lose many of his wealthy customers.

A corrupt Congress party won the first round initiated by Ramdev. It brilliantly used him to sideline its real rival—the BJP. On

1 June 2011, when the media-magnate Baba landed in Delhi to challenge corruption, the Congress dispatched four senior cabinet ministers to meet him at the airport. Pleased with this unexpected honour and official assurances, the Baba (allegedly) signed an agreement to cancel his crusade against corruption. But then, due to some mysterious factor, he changed his mind. Violating his word, he went on a fast-unto-death. His reason for this unexplained behaviour may have been honourable, but it gave credence to the argument that he was using corruption merely to build a political following.

That perception (right or wrong) made people think that the Baba's fast was insincere. Just then, on 4 June, the Congress resuscitated his leadership. After midnight, the Baba was evicted from the Ramlila Grounds. That made him a martyr, compelling Hindutva leaders if they wanted to meet him, to make a pilgrimage to the Baba's Patanjali Yogapeeth in Haridwar.

Civil society, which had been sceptical of the billionaire sannyasi's sincerity, also felt compelled to support him. Anna Hazare went to Mahatma Gandhi's Rajghat to fast in Baba's favour, only to discover that his hero had agreed with Uttarakhand's Chief Minister, Ramesh Pokhriyal Nishank, to give up his fast without forcing upper-caste billionaires to bring their black money back to India. We do not know why the Baba gave up his crusade; some of my intelligent friends made twisted arguments: "It is better for our black money to corrupt the West," or, "it is better for the Baba if the black money returned at election time."

The Baba gave up the first round before finishing the fight. Does his failure make it wiser to follow "civil society"? Sadly, Anna Hazare's "non-political" campaign against corruption is an acknowledgement that (a) secular capitalism has made corruption a bigger problem than Nehruvian *socialism,* and that (b) liberal education, democracy, the judiciary, and the media that created civil society have at the same time also helped to create the current culture that is conducive to corruption. Our so-called secular intelligentsia is simply too prejudiced or closed-minded to investigate the spirituality that successfully fought corruption in the nineteenth century and handed over a clean government to India in 1947.

Anna won our respect because he was not seeking power. Those who remained pessimistic toward his campaign were remembering the JP-led 'Total Revolution' of 1974–75, which climaxed merely in political upheavals of the Emergency (1975–77), the overthrow of Indira Gandhi's Congress, and corrupt misrule by J. P.'s followers.

An "independent" Lokpal (Ombudsman) with authority to hold a prime minister accountable may be a good idea, but hardly new. We already have an "independent" judiciary which convicted Prime Minister Indira Gandhi of electoral corruption. That judgement triggered the chain of events that led to the suspension of the Constitution and detention of thousands of activists who were like Anna Hazare. When a battalion of independent, liberal judges has led to curb corruption, what might enable an individual Lokpal to tackle powerful and well-entrenched evil? What would prevent a corrupt minister from hiring an assassin to get rid of an honest and, therefore, difficult Lokpal?

Ironically, Anna's concerns expose civil society's lack of faith in democracy: Why should anyone believe that an unelected civil society can make corrupt rulers behave morally?

A yogic cure for corruption?

The first time I heard yoga being mentioned in positive terms was in the early 1980s, after Dhirendra Brahmachari became Mrs. Indira Gandhi's personal yoga-teacher. Even then, initially the media ridiculed this trend, which was set by the "hippies." Back then, our cultural attitude to yoga was condescending. It was captured by the 1971 film song "Dum maro dum, mit jaye gum, bolo shubah sham, Hare Krishna, Hare Ram." This attitude was not produced by hippies who loved drugs and free-sex. It was produced by the yogis and tantriks who had been practising spirituality without morality for 2,000 years.

Much has changed during the last four decades. Yoga is now considered a respectable fitness recipe, and no one is exploiting the therapeutic (or, at least the commercial) value of yoga better than Swami Ramdev. Even he, however, does not sell it as a cure for Corruption. This is because corruption is a moral issue, and none of the philosophies that promote yoga diagnose human problems in moral terms. Following the Buddha, Indian philosophers saw our problem as *metaphysical* (ignorance). Therefore, they promote techniques of yoga and meditation for mystical enlightenment that require no commitment to moral purity or rational inquiry. Let me explain:

Some yogic exercises and mysticism existed prior to the Buddha. However, the philosophies that give meaning to yoga became popular mostly after the Buddha. Patanjali's sutras that Ramdev promotes were composed around four hundred years after the Buddha

The sacrificial religion of the Vedas that preceded Gautam Buddha. did consider human sinfulness. It prescribed some animal sacrifice for the forgiveness of our sins. That implied a desire for more change as well as a view that the universe was both a physical as well as a moral system. However, most Vedic sacrifices were intended as bribes to gods to prevent misfortune. Other sacrifices, rituals, and yogic austerities sought favour, power, or revenge on enemies.

Brahminical religion could not inspire followers to seek purity of heart because our gods themselves are unholy and greedy. They do not punish immorality with any consistency. They harass innocent people, creating all sorts of obstacles in their path. Fear of these *obstacles* is the primary reason why Ganesha has to be worshipped before the other gods. He is depicted with a fat belly because of his insatiable appetite for our offerings. Brahmin priests extract offerings from everyone, whether kings or commoners, in the name of our gods. This religiosity became so nauseating that the Buddha reacted against the very idea of gods or God.

As the Buddha rejected God, he could not define the human problem as sin or rebellion against God's moral law. He saw our problem as suffering. His First Noble Truth is demonstrably true: *Life is suffering*. The question is, Why is life suffering? Having sidelined God, to be logically consistent, the Buddha had to reject the notion of soul (atman) in favour of no-soul (anatman). Since free will cannot exist without a soul, the Buddha also had to reject the possibility that a holy God could punish us for sin we "choose" to commit.

Did a Creator then make us suffer because He/She/It is sadistic? Some European contemporaries of the Buddha, called Gnostics, did think that an evil creator made us suffer. But the Buddha could not believe in such a bad God. He came up with the innovative suggestion that our consciousness must have come into existence due to avidya (Primeval Ignorance), karma, and desire. The antidote to Ignorance is Enlightenment, not forgiveness of sin or moral transformation. It made sense that a life filled with suffering was an accidental product of avidya. Assuming that to be the case, the Buddha proposed that we should seek liberation (nirvana) not from sin but from existence itself.

The philosophic traditions and mystical practices, such as yoga and meditation, that followed the Buddha, emphasised mystical (not rational) enlightenment. Of course, some yogic and Buddhist practices required strict adherence to certain ethical conducts, but those conducts were not moral absolutes binding on everyone at all times. They were rules required of practitioners of meditation to help them reach a desired goal. At deeper philosophical levels, our mystical traditions did not believe in a Holy God or moral absolutes, therefore, they did not require all men to repent for moral misdeeds and seek divine forgiveness.

Patanjali Yoga, for example, adopted Samkhya philosophy, which believes in two realities— purusa (soul) and prakruti (matter). Samkhya says that the human predicament is that somehow the soul has become entangled with matter (body). Yoga, in the Samkhya view, is a path of salvation that isolates (kevalyam) soul from body. Seeking out-of-body mystical experiences remains a goal for many yogis even today. However, most teachers now define the human problem in terms of advaita (non-dualism) rather than in the dualism of Samkhya. These teachers of yoga see human misery as caused by the illusion (maya) of the human soul's separation from the divine soul, Brahman. They interpret yoga as an attempt to unite the human self (atman) with the divine self (paramatman). The effort to separate the soul from the illusion-creating body continues, but that is understood as a means and not the end. The end is merging our finite consciousness into a mystical union with the infinite consciousness, Brahman.

Thus, although the dualist and the non-dualist traditions define yoga differently, both follow the Buddha in claiming that the human problem is not moral but metaphysical and, therefore, our salvation requires mystical enlightenment (jnana), not intellectual or moral transformation, that is, turning from myths to truth, or from evil thoughts, words, and deeds to obedience to God, who is loving well as holy.

The Buddhist-Sankhya-Advaita intellectual milieu that governed Indian culture for over 2,000 years did not take sin seriously. Therefore, it precluded the possibility of our liberation from personal sin and social and political slavery, as was accomplished in Europe following the sixteenth-century Protestant Reformation. That comprehensive spiritual, religious, philosophical, political and cultural movement and the spiritual awakenings that followed it created our modern world.

Our philosophy delayed our nation's moral-cultural renewal, so that it could not even begin until the end of the eighteenth century, when Western missionaries, beginning with William Carey, brought to us a biblical view of reality. The Bible accepts the fact that life is suffering, but it reveals that we were created to live in bliss (Eden), not in suffering. Suffering came as a curse upon our sin. And sin is not ignorance but a choice made by free will. It is possible for a soul to sin, because our self, though finite, is not maya. According to the Bible, the spiritual core of our being is real, valuable, and immortal. Because human beings are uniquely precious, the Creator wants to save us from our sin. He is not merely the ultimate judge. God is also our loving Father. While He judges and condemns our sin, it was His love for us that put the curse of human sin upon Jesus the Lord when He was on the cross. The Lord Jesus became the sacrificial lamb.

The Bible reveals that God is determined to save His beautiful creation that has been marred by sin. Although God's will at present is often not done on earth, He will re-establish His reign on earth. All that is sinful will be destroyed, but the earth will be renewed like paradise. It will be bliss again. God is neither corrupt nor capricious. Therefore, God commands us to repent of our sin, seek forgiveness, and become holy like Him, for we were created in His image. We must love our neighbours as ourselves, not covet what belongs to them. The Bible warns that God respects our free will so much that if we persist in choosing to live contrary to will, He respects our choices, and will allow our will to be done so that we are excluded from His grace forever. That is what the Bible calls hell.

The biblical worldview implies hope not only for sinful individuals but also for society as a whole as well as for physical creation. This made sense to Indian reformers such as Raja Ram Mohan Roy, Keshab Chandra Sen, and Mahatma Jotirao Phule. These reformers knew Western missionaries intimately. They could see how their personal lives, even though imperfect, differed so radically from our "saints", as well as from greedy, arrogant Europeans. The reformers were also aware that the biblical worldview has a proven track record of reforming entire nations in Europe and North America. Therefore, like the Buddha, they too mustered up the courage to oppose Brahminical religion that had been developed to exploit and oppress the mass of our people. Great men began opposing Hindu myths, superstitions, idolatry, astrology, untouchability, caste, widow-burning, child-marriage, polygamy, and a whole host of intellectual and social evils. They promoted education for boys and girls, journalism, democracy, and human equality. These builders of modern India are now despised by Brahmin intellectuals because they followed the Bible, albeit only partially. Mahatma Gandhi, Dr. Bhimrao Ambedkar, and Pandit Jawaharlal Nehru continued the reforming tradition initiated by these reformers. The question that we have to face is this:

Why did India's Renaissance create a corrupt culture?

The answer is that Indian reformers were over-optimistic in putting their hope in modern "education" (also pioneered by Western missionaries). In the preface we have, for example, already quoted Mahatma Phule's faith in education. It was lack of education, he said, that lay at the root of our moral and material backwardness.

As it turned out, education divorced from the Bible created graduates who became rich in money but often poorer in morals. Their intellectual prowess, now combined with India's traditional corruption that Phule wrote about, comes up with new arguments and explanations to keep our Bahujan oppressed.

So, what went wrong? The problem was with the idea that ignorance, not sin, constitutes the human problem. However, from Ram Mohan Roy to the early phase of Dr. Ambedkar's training, "ignorance" was understood in terms of Western "Enlightenment" or "Rationalism," that is, lack of information and understanding. This view assumed that human reason could lead people to truth and, therefore, Western-style university education was sufficient to create morally decent "gentlemen," who would create equal opportunity for all. In Mahatma Phule's day, education did create gentlemen. But that happened because all European universities, including state-funded universities, were institutions that still were under the influence of religion. They were established by the Church or monastic orders, though they were granted the authority to operate semi-autonomously, under a bishop. They existed to train young people into godliness. It was only around the year 1900 in Europe and by the 1920s in America that a majority of university professors began to think that the human mind could know truth without God. By the 1950s, they began to come around to agree with the Buddha that the human mind could never find truth by itself (that is, without divine revelation).

The Christian West that Ram Mohan Roy and Phule encountered believed in reason and moral purity because, back then, the West believed that the human self, including the mind, was made in God's image. That made it reasonable to think that the mind's processes, including logic, could lead us to truth and goodness. Now, having rejected the Bible, the West has no choice but to resign itself to myths and mysticism. It is being drawn to Hindu and Buddhist (non-rational) mysticism as well as to corruption. From Rajneesh to Ramdev, many Babas are flourishing, and the postmodern West is going downhill, morally and, therefore, also materially.

Good legislation, education, and democracy are all necessary for building a great India. But it is naive to put faith in a non-moral spirituality, or secularised education and democracy that undermine God's law and grace. Without submission to truth and morality, democracy can and inevitably will become a tyranny terrible for a bullied and bribed "majority." Given our non-moral philosophical culture, there are plenty of reasons why yogi-raj can quickly turn into gunda-raj (rule of the goons).

Just, free, and prosperous political cultures have flourished where individuals, minorities, and majorities have been bound by the righteousness of a holy God. That is why the Lord Jesus asked his followers to first seek, not enlightenment, but the kingdom of God and His righteousness.

Chapter Sixteen

Democracy as Dacoity
The Bandit Queen as Bahujan Hero

All of us are products of the same religio-secular culture that creates the dacoits of Chambal as well as the dacoits of Delhi, Lucknow and Bollywood

In the early 1990s, Manyawar Kanshi Ramji sent me to Gwalior jail to help Phoolan Devi file her nomination papers for Parliament as a BSP candidate. I suspected that since she was still in prison, I may be asked to manage her election campaign also. So, in order to get to know her, I bought a copy of Mala Sen's book, *India's Bandit Queen: The True Story of Phoolan Devi*. Shekhar Kapoor was then turning that book into a feature film. Kapoor's and Sen's self-interest did overshadow their interest in truth. Therefore, as Arundhati Roy predicted (after the film came out), Kapoor's popularisation of Phoolan Devi contributed to her tragic murder in 2001.

However, when I was reading *India's Bandit Queen*, I felt that the book had so much truth about the oppression of backward castes and Indian women that the book deserved to be made required reading for every high school student. It helped me understand why many OBCs were recasting the idols of Devi Durga into the image of Phoolan Devi and why a section of the secular media was turning her into a feminist icon. Oppression is meant to break our spirits; a hero fights back and overcomes. Phoolan Devi was a hero who overcame in real life more than James Bond does on the silver screen. Unfortunately, her heroism was defined by the very culture that keeps us backward. Sadly, I did not get an opportunity to discuss with her our culture's understanding of heroism and genuine heroism.

In Gwalior, I was told that the person who was supposed to have helped Phoolan Devi register as a voter had missed the deadline and so her nomination papers could not be filed. Later, I discovered that I was kept away from her because some people were trying to get Mulayam Singh Yadav to make her a candidate of the Samajwadi party. She preferred that option since it meant that the SP government in Lucknow would not pursue the forty-eight criminal cases against her that included the infamous massacre of twenty-two Thakurs on 14 February, 1981 in Behmai village, where she had earlier been (allegedly) gang raped.

Since many OBCs were worshipping Phoolan Devi as Durga, Kanshi Ram and Mulayam Singh Yadav followed Mala Sen and Shekhar Kapoor in using her for their own ends. Neither of them paused to ask: Has anything reformed Phoolan Devi? However, we cannot blame them because they, like us, are all products of the same religio-secular culture that creates the dacoits of Chambal as well as the dacoits of Delhi, Lucknow and Bollywood. Who pauses to ask: Why do we continue to vote for politicians who loot our money from national, state, city, and village treasuries in *our* name?

The OBCs worshipped Phoolan Devi because she took brutal "revenge" on the Thakurs—most of whom had done her no harm. Likewise, secularists made her an icon of feminism because she took revenge on some men, simply because they were men.

The problem is that the Thakurs did not begin Phoolan's oppression. The OBCs were silent when her father's brother Biharilal and his son (her cousin) Maiyadeen falsified land records, drove her parents out of the family house, and forced them to live in a little hut on the outskirts of the village. Phoolan—a little hero then—took revenge by leading her frightened older sister into her uncle's hora field, munched on their hora nuts, and plucked their flowers. Her cousin Maiyadeen, in his twenties then, ordered the girls off his premises. Instead of obliging, Phoolan questioned his claim to the land and was beaten unconscious with a brick. Standing up against a corrupt cousin was heroic.

Her caste members kept quiet again when Maiyadeen sent

labourers to cut down her father's neem tree. The helpless father saw no point in protesting—our 11-year-old hero did! She staged a sit-in protest (dharna), calling Maiyadeen a thief. Her punishment? Maiyadeen married her off to Putti Lal, three times her age and miles away from her parents.

Phoolan's caste cared neither for her, nor for justice, nor for the law against child marriage. Her husband, Putti Lal (and later his second wife Vidya), took full advantage of her vulnerability. Her family and caste had neither a sense of justice nor compassion when she returned home as an abused woman. It was the head of her own community, Maiyadeen the "thief," who accused her of theft in 1971 and sent her into police custody to be raped and abused for three days and nights. Our police looted her honour as our democratically elected leaders loot *our* money.

Phoolan's spineless community did not care for the little girl and thereby forfeited the right to complain when she reappeared as Durga and made Putti Lal—her husband and fellow member of the Mallah caste—the first target of her revenge. Feminists love to forget that Phoolan avenged herself fully also on her husband's other wife, Vidya. Phoolan hated her and confessed that she wanted to kill both Vidya and Putti Lal but decided to break their bones and leave them alive to tell the story of her "heroic" revenge.

Two Thakurs murdered Phoolan Devi because her heroism involved killing whom she hated, with no desire for their redemption. Her heroism was defined by our gods and goddesses, who become inauspicious to those who do not oblige them, but do nothing to redeem them or draw their hearts to love God.

Without adequate cultural foundations, the best that democracy can do for us is to give power to the Dalits and the OBCs. But power doesn't save: As Lord Acton noted, power corrupts, and absolute power corrupts absolutely. That is why Mahatma Jotirao Phule believed that in order to move forward the heroic saviour that the Bahujans of India need is not a power-seeking politician but a self-sacrificing king: a Baliraja. Phule identified the Baliraja of our mythology with the historical personality, the Lord Jesus, because he understood why Western culture had succeeded in producing leaders who devoted their lives to abolish slave-trade and slavery. He studied the Bible to understand Jesus the Lord.

Like Phoolan Devi, Jesus was also abused by powerful elements in his society. These wolves hated him because he took care of the sheep—the oppressed and the outcastes. Jesus was the good shepherd who sacrificed himself for his helpless sheep. He took the abuses of the oppressed upon him, but asked for forgiveness and transformation for his oppressors. Like Phoolan Devi, Jesus also stood up against the wicked. But his mission was not revenge. He was recognized as the Messiah because He fulfilled the ancient prophecies given by God, through men such as Isaiah, that God's chosen servant will establish justice on this earth. His power will come from the Holy Spirit, not swords or guns:

> "Here is my servant, whom I uphold,
>
> My chosen one in whom I delight;
>
> I will put my Spirit on Him,
>
> and He will bring justice to the nations.
>
> He will not shout or cry out,
>
> or raise His voice in the streets.
>
> A bruised reed He will not break,
>
> and a smouldering wick He will not snuff out.
>
> In faithfulness he will bring forth justice;
>
> He will not falter or be discouraged
>
> till He establishes justice on earth.
>
> In His teaching the islands will put their hope.
>
> This is what God the Lord says—
>
> "I, the Lord, have called you in righteousness;
>
> I will take hold of your hand.
>
> I will keep you and will make you
>
> to be a covenant for the people
>
> and a light for the Gentiles,
>
> to open eyes that are blind,

to free captives from prison
and to release from the dungeon those who sit in darkness."

(Isaiah 42:1-7)

Jesus personified a fearless commitment to justice, but his heroism was different from most other fighters against injustice. He found the power to love His enemies. He was able to bless those who cursed him. That is what converted Saul into Paul—the apostle of love.

Jesus' idea of justice went beyond revenge to include national healing and reconciliation. One of the finest expressions of that ideal was in our own lifetime in South Africa. When I was growing up, it was a nation torn apart by terrible injustices, institutionalised racial discrimination, and hatred known as apartheid. The nation was saved from a bloodbath because Jesus inspired a band of servant leaders (ministers) who dedicated themselves to seeking justice and national reconciliation. They became shepherds who saw their role as taking care of "the bruised reed and flickering flames." But our little, abused, and brave 11-year-old Mallah girl, Phoolan, lacked models who could have made her a hero that really deserved emulation in the first place and, in the second place, emulating who might have helped transform our nation.

Chapter Seventeen
Rahul to Gandhi
"What kind of a leader should India have?

The revolutionary idea that a ruler should be a servant developed only after Europe rejected Machiavelli's mindset.

On 21 August 2010, the Prime Minister-in-Waiting, 40-year-old Rahul Gandhi, displayed impressive political aptitude. In pouring rain, he drove 110 kilometres to pay a surprise visit to some UP farmers. They were agitated because the government of UP was acquiring their only source of livelihood—their fertile land—and planning to build, partly on them, the 165-km Yamuna Expressway to make it possible to travel from Noida to Agra in ninety minutes. Farmers are upset about the inadequate and unjust compensation: Losing their inter-generational source of livelihood, the farmers are unlikely to be able to live on the compensation during the period they need to find fresh means of earning a living. The road will certainly boost tourism, trade, and industry, but only the resourceful will benefit. Most of those who are already poor will lose whatever means they have of earning a living.

Rahul's Gandhigiri

Rahul shocked the media and political rivals as he stole the limelight from Ajit Singh to make sure that the latter did not remain the sole champion of Western UP's farmers. In the same visit, Rahul also made an emotional dent into Chief Minister Mayawati's Dalit base by visiting the families of two innocent Dalits who were killed when Mayawati's police opened fire on protesting farmers.

Earlier, Rahul and his mother, Mrs. Sonia Gandhi—the powerful fourth-term president of the ruling Congress party—had taken a stand in favour of Orissa's tribals, who (backed by Maoists) were resisting efforts by Vedanta, a multinational company, to acquire their lands for mining. By championing the victims of modern development, was Rahul trying to ensure that when his government, headed by Prime Minister Manmohan Singh, does pass a new land-acquisition law, it will not hurt him electorally? Does he hope that green activists and the global media will project him favourably when the poor are forced to yield their lands anyway?

Rahul Gandhi is a public figure, but his world of private thoughts and policies is still a mystery. Potentially, he could influence the next three decades of our national life. Therefore, it is interesting to probe the secrets of his mind.

***

Desh ka neta kaisa ho?

Imagine that after returning from his triumphant trip to UP, Rahul tried reading a few pages from Mahatma Gandhi's latest biography, but found that he was too tired. So, he turned on the TV to see how the media was covering his tour. What pleased him the most was his followers' chant, "Desh ka neta kaisa ho? Rahul Gandhi Jaisa ho" (What kind of a leader should the country have? He should be like Rahul Gandhi.) However, as he flipped channels, he was irritated that in another part of UP, Mayawati was unveiling a statue of her mentor, Kanshi Ram, and a much bigger crowd was chanting, "Desh ka neta kaisa ho? Mayawati jaisa ho" (The country's leader should be like Mayawati).

Staring at Bapu's portrait on the cover of the biography still in his hands, a sleepy Rahul took a deep breath, and murmured to the Mahatma:

What kind of a leader *should* India have?

While drifting into a well-earned sleep, he felt that Bapu's smile was coming alive. In fact, Bapu's ghost emerged out of the book and sat down on his bed, looking at him with compassion such as a grandfather may have for a baby sleeping in his arms. Beta (son)!— Bapu said kindly—You were born great; Mayawati has achieved greatness; while greatness was thrust upon your mother. She has handled power fairly wisely, what Mayawati and you will do with your power is yet to be seen. Much of your contribution to India will depend on circumstances that you will not be able to control, but history will judge Mayawati and you by the choices you make. Your private and public decisions will show the strength or weakness of your inner characters.

But Mayawati is so corrupt! said Rahul, as he didn't relish being classed together with her.

Sadly, the Mahatma said gently, the truth is that if your family must get the credit for keeping Mother India a democracy, then it must also share the blame for the moral degeneration of her public life.

Do you really think that my family is a key to India's success as a democracy? Rahul tried to steer the conversation in a positive direction.

Of course! said the Mahatma with his usual twisted smile. The only "ideologies" that define our two-coalition system is loyalty or hatred for the ruling dynasty. Other than that, our political class is driven by nothing but a lust for power.

Isn't politics just about power?

But isn't politics about power—acquiring it and retaining it?

That is what Machiavelli taught in his book, *The Prince*. As an Italian diplomat, he was able to study many fifteenth-century European rulers, those who succeeded and those who lost power. He also studied ancient rulers and political philosophers, and taught the kind of politics that he could have learned from our own Chanakya. Our rulers were experts in the art of acquiring and retaining political power. Sons routinely killed their fathers and brothers for the throne. Even Kaikeyi succeeded in sending Ram into exile and making her own son the ruler of Ayodhya. The tragedy is that during your dynasty's rule, although not because of it, Indian politics has been degenerating into its traditional Machiavellian, understanding of politics as power. The rhetoric of principles has become only a means to power.

What else can politics be, if it is not about power?

I'm sure you've heard some of the speeches of your great-grandfather. Jawahar never missed an opportunity to teach the nation that he was their First Servant; for that is what 'Prime Minister' literally means. This revolutionary idea that a ruler should be a servant developed only after Europe rejected Machiavelli's mindset. Beginning with some Huguenots in France, Scottish, English, and Dutch reformers began asking: What kind of rulers does God want us to have? They read the Bible with that question in mind because they believed that the Bible was God's perspective on Jewish and world history. When they decided to learn politics from God's perspective, they began to understand Jesus Christ and his teaching that ungodly rulers, including in Europe, lorded it over their subjects; but God is inaugurating a new kingdom in which whoever wants to be great must become a servant. Jesus said that although he was the Jewish Messiah, he had come, not to be served but to serve and give his life for the liberation of others. That is why the cross on which he died has become the most powerful global symbol of self-sacrificing service.

Jawahar was a historian. He saw plenty of racism and class discrimination in England. India was fortunate that Jawahar also saw the beauty of the Bible's teaching on leadership and governance. He practised it by honouring his critics, such as Dr. Ambedkar. Yet, his generation made the big mistake of thinking that good leaders could grow in every soil. To say that he studied in England is to say that Jawahar grew in biblical soil. Time has shown that servant-leaders don't grow in soils that lack the nutrients derived from the Bible.

European nations such as Scotland, England, Holland, and Switzerland became models of democracy only because they rejected Machiavellian realism. They allowed an Asian book—the Bible—to define politics. Our problem is that although we were humble enough to imitate Western democracies, we have been too arrogant to open our hearts to the spirituality needed to make democracy work. What do you think will happen to Indian democracy if your family was suddenly removed by an accident?

The Congress will disintegrate for sure.

Also, the opposition to Congress will disintegrate. The two-coalition system that has given some stability and created the illusion of democratic success will collapse. How strong is a democracy that depends on a dynasty for its very survival? The Hindutva party has got a few things right, but it lacks humility to acknowledge that just as Europe needed Reformation, so does India. For real success, Indian democracy needs transformation, not preservation of its immoral culture. You can be grateful your dynasty has played a role, but you will need enormous inner spiritual resources to really change India.

Bapu! Many of my teachers say that Panditji didn't follow you all the way because he thought that some of your idealism was crazy.

They are right, and so was Jawahar. I did think a lot of crazy thoughts and did do a lot of stupid things. Therefore, only someone crazy will follow everything I said or did. But intelligent sceptics like your great-grandfather followed me, gave up everything, spent years in jails, and became willing to die for the nation because they knew that neither I nor the Congress party that I led was corrupt. Modern India was born only because Providence did not allow our character to be shaped by Machiavelli, Chanakya, or our gods and epics. In our generation, the educated class allowed the Bible to shape important aspects of our character, such as integrity and self-sacrificing service. That explains the generational difference between our generation and yours. You may be good. Your problem, however, is: can you find enough good politicians and bureaucrats to govern the country? Jawahar thought that his Five-Year Plans would make India a manufacturing giant, but he did little to make sure that India nurtures godly character to manage his projects.

You were trained as a lawyer, so I shouldn't even try to argue with you. In any case, your comments about India's moral degeneration are sadly true. The UP government has never been more corrupt than under Mayawati, and look there, on that channel, our people are still chanting, "Desh ka neta kaisa ho, Mayawati jaisa ho."

This is not about winning or losing an argument. The question is: Do you want to be a smarter politician than Mayawati or qualitatively different and better?

What do you mean?

The drama that you staged in UP today was brilliant. You can outsmart Maya, Mulayam, and Ajit. That will make you the prime minister, but it will not change India.

Gandhi to Rahul: Try servant-leadership

So what do you think I should do?

Do you really want my advice?

I do. I want to know what kind of a leader India should have. You are asking for trouble, beta. But since you've asked, I will tell you what you can do to change India. If you really care for the corruption, pollution, or the poverty in UP, then apply to the electorate to appoint you as the Chief Servant of UP.

That is crazy. How can our party win UP? We are number four, behind BSP, SP, and the BJP.

You can win UP without fighting for it. Humble yourself. Make an honest, public offer to Mayawati that you will do everything you can to make her the next prime minister of India. In return, you seek her help in getting elected as the Chief Servant of UP. Tell her that you will select the best available candidates for UP's state legislature, irrespective of their caste and present party affiliations. That she should campaign for you and your party and that you will campaign for her during the national elections. Tell her and the people of UP that you want UP to teach you how to govern. After you have proven yourself in UP, then you will ask the nation to give you the opportunity to serve as its First Servant.

You know Bapu, that the Congress party will never allow me to become the chief minister of UP. If I fail there, it will hurt the entire party. Are you a follower or a leader of the Congress party?

Are you in politics to serve the interests of your party members? By taking up the responsibility of cleaning up UP, you will become a game-changer, a politician who is truly a class apart from Mayawati as well as from your own father and grandmother. In one stroke, you will win back the vote banks, including the Dalits that have been lost due to Congress' hypocrisy.

Chapter Eighteen
Where Are Our Heroes?

Political power is necessary. Yet, by itself it will reduce our heroes to netas, unless we find the Saviour who can transform our hearts, character and worldview.

Mannu was once a hero, now he is a neta - an MLA in UP. When I first met him in early 1988, he was only about twenty years old but already highly respected in two districts. He had cycled from village to village and town to town and awakened a sleeping giant—the Bahujan—to its political potential.

Mannu (not his real name) came from a Scheduled Caste family, but he was honoured by educated OBCs and Muslims because he was sincere in his belief that there is no need for India's oppressed to remain backward. He hammered home the message that democracy has made it possible for them to change our 3,000-year-old history. Therefore, they should move forward. The Bahujans are 85 percent of India and have the power to vote their own people to the highest offices. Political power, he pointed out, will be the key to economic, social, and educational development.

Mannu's parents thought that he was wasting his life. They advised him to go to college and get a job, without which he could not get a good wife. Mannu had nothing to support him in his mission except his faith, his power to persuade others, and the encouragement of a few government employees from Scheduled Caste backgrounds. They believed in him and, once in a while, helped him financially. Mannu risked his personal future for the public good. Through his tenacious and focused hard work, he succeeded in mobilising about a hundred people from his district to travel to Allahabad the summer of 1988 to campaign for his then largely unknown hero, Kanshi Ram. The latter had the audacity to run for Parliament against joint opposition candidate, V. P. Singh, and against Sunil Shastri, son of the late prime minister Lal Bahadur Shastri, who had been handpicked by Rajiv Gandhi. Kanshi Ram taught the oppressed in Allahabad that both these candidates represented India's hierarchical, Brahminical culture, therefore, Dalit-Bahujans should not vote to sustain the status quo.

My friend Jebaraj and I teamed up with Mannu in campaigning for Kanshi Ram in that historic parliamentary by-election, which paved the way for V. P. Singh to become the prime minister of India and later, for Mayawati to capture Lucknow, as well as for Mannu to become a Member of Legislative Assembly.

Our candidate, Kanshi Ram, came third in Allahabad. However, his campaign planted the seeds of a socio-spiritual ferment that went far beyond politics.

The Rise of Kanshi Ram

Mannu became a hero by believing and following Manyawar Kanshi Ramji. The latter inspired Mannu's dedication and missionary spirit because Kanshi Ramji gave up the kind of life Mannu's parents wanted him to seek a secure job as an officer of the Government of India. Kanshi Ram sacrificed the respect and financial security of his job to dedicate his life to transform India by empowering its oppressed Bahujan population. Manyawar Kanshi Ramji was born on 15 March 1934 in Ropar district of Punjab, in a Scheduled Caste family that had converted to Sikhism. He died on 9 October 2006 in New Delhi. Kanshi Ram's abilities got him a job as a civil servant under the quota reserved for the Scheduled Castes. Dr. Ambedkar's writings, however, inspired him to quit his job. For eight years he then volunteered in Maharashtra as a foot soldier of the Republican Party of India. That party had been established to fulfil the dreams of Babasaheb Dr. Bhimrao Ambedkar, but petty personal ambitions of leaders kept splitting it up. Kanshi Ram began to get disillusioned, and the last straw came when the biggest Ambedkarite leader of the Republican Party struck a deal to support the Congress party in exchange for one seat in Parliament and a few lakh rupees. Kanshi Ram felt that this leader had bartered the party's mission and sacrifices of faithful workers for his own immediate interests. Realising that Ambedkarism's political ideals did not have the spiritual power to actually change India, Kanshi Ram established the Buddhist Research Foundation to study if Babasaheb's religion could save the Backwards (Dalit-Bahujan).

A careful study of Buddhism and the actual life of the neo-Buddhist monks helped Kanshi Ram understand why Buddhism had failed in ancient India and made little difference in the lives of modern neo-Buddhists in Maharashtra. A realisation that both Ambedkar's political as well as religious visions, had led to dead ends could have discouraged an ordinary person; but Kanshi Ram was a hero, and heroes don't give up.

In search of a winning strategy, Kanshi Ram relocated to New Delhi. As he met with Scheduled Caste employees, he realised that even though the Phule-Ambedkar movement had failed in Maharashtra, Dr. Ambedkar himself was held in great respect. Kanshi Ram had become an expert on Ambedkar, whose books and work had inspired him at the start of his public life. He turned his knowledge into an asset and decided to capitalise on Ambedkar's growing popularity among SCs and other Bahujans. He began teaching that the Scheduled Caste employees were the beneficiaries of a social revolution started by Mahatma Phule and Dr. Ambedkar, and therefore, they ought to support his Ambedkarite mission.

Of course, Kanshi Ram frequently acknowledged that, in fact, it was Jesus Christ and his followers who had started India's social revolution. Yet, since he had never investigated why Jesus and the Bible had been changing the world for 2,000 years, his understanding of global and Indian histories was relatively poor. Promoting Ambedkar as an icon was enough to raise support for his dream to snatch power from the upper castes. Mannu's faith in Kanshi Ram was so strong that he could not see the clear signals that Kanshi Ram's private actions contradicted his public mission to empower the oppressed. Let me explain:

Kanshi Ram was a hero because he was willing to fight for his mission and lose. After losing many elections, he won a seat in Parliament only twice. The second of which was only for a brief period (1996-97). Likewise, BSP's only other leader, Mayawati, lost in elections in 1984 (Kairana), in 1985 (Bijnor), and again in 1987 (Haridwar). This string of losses would have discouraged most people, yet, inspired and encouraged by Kanshi Ram, she did not give up. Finally, she won in Bijnor in 1989. In that same election, two other BSP candidates won parliamentary seats from Rewa (MP), and Jalandhar (Punjab). Mannu and I were there in New Delhi to celebrate this maiden victory on the spacious lawns of Kanshi Ram's bungalow that Prime Minister Chandrashekhar had allotted to him.

Achilles' heel of our Bahujan leaders

Kanshi Ram asked me to prepare the lawn for the celebration. I set up four chairs, one for him and three for our MPs. After party activists had assembled on the lawns, Kanshi Ram came out, looked at the four chairs, and asked me to remove two of them. Only he and Mayawati were to sit on the chairs! The MPs, he felt, owed his victory to him; therefore, they needed to sit at his feet!

Personally, I was content to sit at Kanshi Ram's feet. But treating our newly elected Members of Parliament with such contempt troubled me. I thought the BSP was about restoring the dignity to the oppressed, and our MPs represented people who had been forced for thousands of years to sit at the feet of the upper castes. I had assumed that a true hero was like Jesus, who washed the feet of his disciples—simple folk, like fishermen.

It took me years to understand that Kanshi Ram kept BSP leaders under his feet because of what he had seen in the Ambedkarite movement in Maharashtra. It was "leaders" of the Republican 106 Party that had split it again and again. Therefore, Kanshi Ram did not want leaders in BSP—he only wanted slaves. He wanted to transform India, but he had no clue on how to transform his own disciples; how to ensure that power will not corrupt them; that they will not be bought by rival parties; that they will pursue power for the people, not for themselves.

Mannu's faith in Kanshi Ram had inspired his heroism. Unfortunately, his faith also blinded him. He could not see what became obvious to me. Perhaps one illustration is sufficient to make the point. A few years after we had become friends, Mannu got very angry with me because the UP BSP's chief, Raj Bahadur, and I objected to the way Kanshi Ram was treating Mayawati—our respected Behanji. Special elections were being held in Punjab at the height of Khalistani terrorism. Kanshi Ramji asked me to shadow and chauffeur Ms. Mayawati twenty-four hours a day because she was our candidate for Parliament. He moved in to live with a younger backward-caste woman. Her husband—a government servant—wanted Kanshi Ram to make his wife the "Mayawati of Punjab." So, with mutual consent, during the election period he went to another city while Kanshi Ram moved into his home.

Mayawati hated Kanshi Ram's relations with this and other women. For him, however, this was a part of India's brahmacharya culture. Not marrying a wife gives them the right to everyone else's wife. Over time, I came to realize that Kanshi Ram slept with other women, in part to crush Ms. Mayawati's ego, and keep her insecure and dependent.

Didn't five Pandavs share one wife, Draupadi? Didn't "Dharm Yudhishthir gamble her away to be humiliated in public by Duryodhan? Didn't Krishna, who saved Draupadi, flirt with Gopis? The idea that a man and a woman should have an exclusive and loyal relationship as husband and wife was not an Indian ideal—certainly not for Kanshi Ram nor for Mahatma Gandhi.

Be that as it may, that occasion was different. It was more than Kanshi Ram sleeping with another woman. Mayawati realized that if this attractive, young, Sikh OBC woman won the election, then there would be three chairs in the BSP! So, she began to protest the inappropriateness of Kanshi Ram's "infidelity."

In order to embarrass Kanshi Ram, she announced that she was quitting the election battle. She asked me to drive her back to Delhi. I agreed with her that it was wrong for Kanshi Ramji to sleep with another woman, but I didn't think that she should quit. Therefore, in Raj Bahadur's presence, I respectfully confronted Kanshi Ramji: "Mayawati is not simply a woman in love with you. She is also a symbol of our struggle. As a Dalit woman, she is the lowest of the low. You took a revolutionary step in making a woman, a Dalit, our leader in Parliament when we had three MPs, including two men. That was a wonderful public statement that the BSP stands for the lowest of the low. You live with her in Delhi; therefore, you are violating dignity by sleeping with another woman. This is a terrible model for hundreds of party activists here who look up to you as a model."

Happily, Kanshi Ram listened to me and reorganised housing. He moved into the hotel where the BSP men were staying, and Mayawati stayed with her brother and sister-in-law. Nevertheless, the public fight between the two women candidates cost us both the seats. After the elections, Kanshi Ramji decided that he did not want followers like me who had the audacity to stand up to him. He wanted people like Mannu, who would obey him, no matter what. Mannu—a champion of the oppressed—had no moral framework with which to judge if it was wrong for Kanshi Ram to have relations with whichever woman he wanted. It is also possible that Mannu was clever and did not want to offend the other woman who had become Kanshi Ram's favourite mistress for the moment. She was potentially the next party leader.

I continued looking up to Mannu as a hero, but once Mayawati became BSP's sole leader, she treated him like dirt—exactly, as Kanshi Ram had often treated her. By then Mannu had no place to go. He was forced to let go of his idealism and replace it with political pragmatism. He ceased being a hero—a man with a mission. He became a neta, making other Dalits touch his feet and beg favours from him.

The limits of politics and power

Mannu knows that UP's Dalit revolution was inspired by Periyar's Dravidian revolution in Tamil Nadu. However, while anti-

Brahmanism has been a potent mantra to dethrone Brahminical parties, it lacked power to transform Indian character. Political power so corrupted the Dravidian movement that Tamil Nadu's Dalit Bahujan repeatedly voted to elect a Dravidian's Brahmin mistress as the state's chief minister. Mannu also knows that just as the Brahmins of UP ditched the BJP, they would also ditch Mayawati. In fact, he is smart enough to know that even the Dalits will ditch a leader who uses them to acquire power and then treats them like dirt. This makes Mannu insecure. In turn, insecurity about BSP's future forces former heroes like him to squeeze out as much public money for themselves as they can, in as short a period as possible. In fact, Mannu is quite aware that his party's corruption is eroding people's confidence in democracy itself. Democracy indeed has the power to change governments. It gave an "untouchable" young man like Mannu the opportunity to develop his talents and become a leader. But it has little power to change people. One of Mannu's colleagues was recently arrested for raping a minor. Mannu's own heroism has disappeared. Is it partly because his own hero, Kanshi Ram, gave him no talisman to transform Indian character? Without godly character, will lower caste netas behave just like the upper caste netas, trampling others under their feet, looting public funds, raping vulnerable women, and murdering rivals? Is it possible that we remain backward because we have no saviour who will deliver us from our sin, including from the corrupting influence of our traditional culture?

Political power is necessary. Yet, by itself, it will reduce our heroes to netas, unless we find the Saviour who can transform our hearts, character, and worldview.

Chapter Nineteen
Will Bahujan's Corrupt Democracy?

Since the Bahujan movement has acquired the maturity to allow honest in-house debate, I have the freedom to say that the Dravidian-Bahujan movement is being destroyed by the corruption of our leaders. Our movement has proven itself incapable of cultivating morally upright leadership.

Why was the 43-year-old DMK Member of Parliament, Ms. Kanimozhi, sent to Tihar Jail on 13 May 2011? The allegation, of course, is corruption. But why didn't she get bail? Is it possible that she was sent to jail because the Congress party has decided to complete what voters began— finish off the DMK to create political space for the state Congress party in Tamil Nadu?

Ms. Kanimozhi is the favourite daughter of Karunanidhi, the Dravidian chief minister. She is now rejected by Dravidian voters as "corrupt." A published poet, Ms. Kanimozhi has a master's degree in economics, worked as a journalist for several publications, and ran a website before joining active politics. Kanimozhi is the sophisticated and urbane Delhi face of Dravidian politics, who shared her father's love of writing Tamil literature, while also talking the language of the GenNext.

Ms. Kanimozhi is said to be the political heavyweight behind Manmohan Singh's decision to appoint the Dalit leader, A. Raja, as the telecom minister. It was alleged that she took Rs 2.14- billion bribe in the 2G (Second-Generation Spectrum) scandal via Kalaignar TV, in which she held a 20 percent stake. Her alleged nominee, "The Raja of Corruption," who was put in Tihar jail until acquitted by the courts as alleged to have collected Rs 30-billion (approx. $8 billion) in that scam. A small portion of this black money was, allegedly, laundered through associate Sadiq Batcha's businesses. Before the CBI could finish investigating Batcha, his dead body was found hanging at his home in Chennai with an apparent suicide note. The investigative agencies could not prove the scandal. Yet, at that time it seemed so big that more "suicides" and murders seemed plausible, as my former friend, (then) Janata Party's president, Subramaniam Swamy, said. However, with due respect to Swamy ji, it will be naive to doubt that it was the Brahmin-Bania PR machine that fooled TIME Magazine into labelling A. Raja as the "biggest global abuser of power," second only to the disgraced American president, Richard Nixon. There is no way Raja could have pocketed $8 billion. Whatever the actual amount of the loot, he would have had to share it with his superiors and subordinates. The complaint that his decision to charge a lower licence fee (2001 rate in 2008) cost the government around $40 billion is clearly motivated. If he had issued those licences to established businesses owned by the upper-caste elite, they may well have voted to make him the prime minister of India. They would have showered much bigger bribes upon him than he got from the small businesses that he favoured. The decision to charge a lower fee to enable small, upcoming businesses to venture into telecom simply meant that his ministry (central government) "subsidized" newcomers to the telecom industry. Every government does that with many sectors of the economy all the time. Not taxing agriculture, for example, means that the government chooses to lose hundreds of billions of dollars every year.

Taking bribes is terrible, but Raja's attempt to break the monopoly of established mega-businesses by bringing new players into the telecom sector is a good thing for the consumer and the nation. The TIME reporter was deceived by the upper-caste elite because, according to the best estimates accepted even by L. K. Advani, upper-caste politicians, businessmen, and bureaucrats are hiding a least $1,500 billion of black money in secret Swiss accounts alone. That is around two hundred times more than the amount of which A. Raja is accused. There can be no doubt that the amount of upper caste's black money within India and in the two hundred tax havens around the world is many times more than what is kept in secret accounts in Switzerland alone.

Before you misunderstand me, let me state categorically that I am not advancing arguments to defend Raja and his patrons. I am empathising with the sentiments of those Dalit-Bahujan intellectuals who feel that the moral "crusade" against Raja has little to do with a desire to eradicate corruption from our public life; that the current war against a Dravidian party is being waged by upper-caste businessmen, media, and parties who oppose Dalit-Bahujan power mainly because Raja favoured small and unknown businessmen. I wish that Raja and Kanimozhi had taken an open and public stand that 2G licenses will not be allotted to established business houses; that they will be given—without bribes—to qualified businessmen (largely, but not exclusively) from castes that do not have a family tradition of business. Such a public stance would have been contested politically and legally, but that is a battle worth fighting. Even if they lost the battle, the DMK would have earned the right to lead the nation.

The foregoing is a lengthy introduction to my main point: the Dalit Bahujan sentiment expressed above has merit. However, it will be foolish to see only the enemy outside while avoiding facing the more important question: True, so far, it is the upper-caste elite who have corrupted democracy, but is all the evidence not that our Bahujan can corrupt democracy even more?

Democracy is a philosophical-sociological force that is transforming India. It is enabling our lower castes to capture political power and to use that power to democratize knowledge, industry, business, media, and wealth. In a sense, Karunanidhi, Kanimozhi, Raja, Mayawati, Lalu Prasad, or Mulayam Singh were/are attempting that kind of a historic transformation... yet, while they fought Brahminism, they could not resist the seduction of sin. Instead of using their power to serve the weak, they abused it to also serve themselves. Thus, it is not the upper-caste media or parties alone that are destroying Dravidian-Bahujan movements, the real enemy is our own sinfulness.

Since the Bahujan movement has acquired the maturity to allow honest in-house debate, I have the freedom to say that the Dravidian-Bahujan movement is being destroyed by the corruption of our leaders. Our movement has proven itself incapable of cultivating morally upright leadership. One main reason is that the pioneers of the modern Bahujan movement, such as Periyar and Kanshi Ram, did not even acknowledge the reality of sin. They were so busy saving us from Brahminism that they did not think about saving us from our own sinfulness. E. V. Ramasamy Periyar, the great grandfather of the disgraced DMK, was right in rejecting Hinduism as myth. But unfortunately, he fell prey to an equally corrupting myth: Western atheism.

Like the Buddha and Jotiba Phule, Periyar was right in perceiving that Brahmins had invented mythical gods and goddesses of Hinduism in order to perpetuate a "dharma" that suited their vested interests. But the Buddha's so-called "atheism" was different from Periyar's or Kanshi Ram's. Buddha simply rejected man-made gods. He was silent about whether a Creator God exists. He was wise enough to know that by itself the human mind cannot know the ultimate reality. However, the inability of the human reason to discover ultimate reality does not mean that we should succumb to myths and superstitions. What is a myth? The term myth has many meanings: I am using the term to mean a view of reality that is invented by the human mind with an ulterior motive. A scientific theory is also invented by the human mind, but it seeks to interpret observed data without ulterior motives. Ideally, science pursues truth wherever it leads, to one's advantage or disadvantage. Given the fact that human beings are sinful, it is possible for a scientist or a group of scientists to develop a theory (say, of global warming) with an ulterior motive (say, to prevent Chinese and Indians from using cheap, carbon-based energy such as coal).

An honest scientific theory may also turn out to be a myth with terrible consequences. That is what happened to Darwin's theory of evolution. The Nazis used it to defend human inequality because it was and is held to imply that some human beings might be more evolved than others. The Nazi argument was (a) that the Aryans ought to rule the world because they have evolved the most, (b) that the "survival of the fittest" means that compassion for the unfit—for example, the handicapped—is wrong, and (c) the cultural and racial Other, the Jew, must not be allowed to succeed in business or in life. On the basis of Nazi-type thinking, it would be possible to conclude, in the case of A. Raja's actions, that preference for small businessmen must be quashed.

Brahmins did invent their myths to control and exploit the masses. But A. Raja, Kanimozhi, and the DMK party are victims of Periyar's atheism, which is also a myth.

Atheism is a myth because

- It is an interpretation of reality (cosmos) that is invented by the human mind and

- It is invented in the absence of scientific data that compels anyone to that conclusion.

Atheists can't prove God's non-existence. They *believe* in the Creator's non-existence because of ulterior motives. Some want to free themselves from the moral demands of a holy God. This was true of Kanshi Ram. He did not want a God who would command, 'You shall not covet your neighbour's wife." This is not meant to be a personal attack on an individual. The point is that atheism, like Hinduism, is a myth created to cultivate corruption. Western atheists did not want to live under a God who says, "You shall not commit adultery." Indian atheists do not like a God who says, "You shall not covet" or "steal" public funds.

Like the Buddha, Scottish Rationalist David Hume understood that logic cannot prove God or science. There is no way one can go around proving empirically that water will boil at 100 degrees Celsius everywhere in the universe under the same atmospheric pressure. Uniformity of natural causes is actually a theological axiom resting on the Bible's teaching that one God created the entire cosmos; therefore, all of it is regulated by His word.

In James Cameron's film, *Avatar*, mountains hang upside down because his moon, Pandora, is a living being, a goddess, just like the earth. She can choose to have mountains controlled by anti-gravity while the earth functions on gravity. While Hume was right in arguing that Reason cannot prove God or science, he made the mistake of thinking that rationality could make us moral without God.

German philosopher Immanuel Kant demonstrated that by itself logic cannot prove morality. Does that mean that God, science, and morality are not true? Yes, but only if you insist that you will believe only what logic can prove. But why do you believe that the universe is logical or that truth has to be logical? Why should the universe be logical, if there is no Creator who is a rational being? That is, if the verse is a product of random (non-rational) chance or Ignorance (Avidya) as the Buddha thought? The Buddha was wise. He realised that those who reject God have to reject reason as the road to enlightenment. They have to meditate to silence their thoughts—to stop thinking.

The Bible promotes education and established universities because it asks us to seek truth, know truth, and believe only what is true. It asks us to put our trust in a God who, though He is beyond our rationality, is nevertheless rational, and has created a world that is understandable through reason, because He has made us like Himself—that is, rational. Of course, we are not merely rational, but the Bible teaches that our minds can know the truth because God has revealed it to us in His word (the Bible) and in His works manifest in nature and culture. Neither nature nor culture is divine. There is plenty of evil in nature and in culture. Yet, both nature and culture bear witness to God's goodness and greatness. Our rationality is valid because it is the means of studying the book of God's words and his works. Modern science was born when rational principles (or logic) which were used to study the God's Word began to be used to study God's works.

Rationality is God given and necessary. *Rationalism*, in contrast, was an arrogant philosophical movement that thought that one could know the truth by studying nature and culture without the light of revelation. Rationalism ended when Western philosophers realized, as did the Buddha, that there is no reason to trust reason. Once you understand the intellectual tragedy of the contemporary West, it becomes easy to grasp, how intelligent crusaders such as Periyar and Arun Shourie ended up as atheists, confirming that (without divine revelation) the human mind cannot know the truth. Arun Shourie described himself as an atheist who is an ardent idol worshipper.

Atheism is a term that describes what a person does not believe; it does not tell us if he knows what is true. To believe in nothing is simply an admission that you do not know the truth. To be a theist may be honest about one's ignorance of truth. But to be ignorant and to insist that God cannot exist or cannot reveal the truth to anyone is simply foolish arrogance.

What does the "fact" mean that logic cannot prove God, science, or morality? Does it mean that God does not exist and morality is meaningless? Or, does it mean that human logic is limited? If a God does exist, can He reveal Himself to us?

Can we communicate the truth to each other? If "yes," then why can't God reveal truth to us? Why can't He tell us that good and evil are real and that He will punish evil but that He can also save us from sin?

Because atheism cannot promote moral absolutes, its spread means that democracy, capitalism, universities, law, medicine, media, sports, and even scientific institutions are becoming corrupt, even in Western countries such as the USA. A scientist in one of our universities told me that he awards PhDs to researchers under him, but he does not believe their data. They fudge their research because much of the time their instruments don't work. Even when they do work, students may not be meticulous in their work.

It was not democracy that gave a clean government to Britain or colonial India. Two hundred years ago, the British Parliament was a gentleman's club, run for the benefit of the club members. Lords and MPs owned the companies that sold African slaves in the

Americas and the Caribbean. Britain was freed from such institutionalized evils because great men such as William Wilberforce fought for decades to bring Britain's public institutions under the moral authority of God's revelation in the Bible.

From 1793 to 1813, Wilberforce also campaigned to force the British East India Company to educate Indians to make them capable of governing themselves as citizens. Lord Thomas Babington Macaulay grew up in Wilberforce's community called "the Clapham Circle." He continued his predecessor's battles. The "Macaulay Minute," which lies at the root of India's current success, is well known, but not many people know that he also fought and won the battle to ensure that the Indian Civil Service (ICS, which became IAS), would be recruited on the basis of merit and not bribes. Britain itself followed his scheme only after India began training and recruiting an honest bureaucracy. In his magisterial study, *Call to Seriousness: The Evangelical Impact on the Victorians*, historian Ian Bradley documents how God's self-revelation in the Bible created clean politics and bureaucracy in Britain and its colonies, including India, through the British Evangelical movement.

Atheism is a myth that was invented to corrupt the kind of character that can develop when individuals and societies genuinely respect, love, and trust God. Playwright-politician Vaclav Havel has documented how the myth of atheism corrupted the former communist countries. Our Bahujan need to be freed from Brahminical myths, organizations, political parties, businesses, and media... but the latest 2G tragedy of the DMK tells us that, above everything else, we need God's power to save us from our sin.

In some ways, the "Raja of corruption" is a victim of an "upper-caste conspiracy." Even if that is the case, they were able to throw him into prison only because, when it comes to corruption, the Bahujan politicians resemble their upper-caste counterparts. India needs public figures who will be prepared to suffer for being righteous.

PART VI

THE HOPE

Chapter Twenty
Nobel Prize for Love

Our professional culture is such that if your superiors suspect that you might outshine them in a field where they have worked for decades, they will go out of their way to create hurdles for you, just as some of our gods become inauspicious to you simply because you haven't fed their insatiable appetite and ego.

When President Barack Obama received the Nobel Prize for Peace in a prestigious ceremony at the beautiful Concert Hall in Stockholm, Sweden, on 10 December 2009, India-born Venkatraman (Venki) Ramakrishnan was also one of nine scientists honoured with Nobel Prizes for their contributions to humanity.

Venki, an American citizen who works at the MRC Laboratory of Molecular Biology in Cambridge, England, was born in Chidambaram in Cuddalore district of Tamil Nadu and graduated from the Maharaja Sayajirao University of Baroda. He shared the Nobel Prize for Chemistry with fellow American Thomas Steitz and Israel's Ada Yonath—the first woman to receive the prize since 1964. Together, the three of them created detailed blueprints of ribosomes —the protein-making machinery within cells. Their research is being used to develop new antibiotics.

The Nobel Prize in physiology or medicine is being shared by three Americans: Elizabeth H. Blackburn, Carol W. Greider, and Jack W. Szostak. They discovered how chromosomes protect themselves as cells divide. Their work has inspired experimental cancer therapies and may offer insights into ageing.

The Nobel Prize in physics will also be given to three Americans: Charles K. Kao, Willard S. Boyle, and George E. Smith. Kao discovered how to transmit light signals long distance through hair-thin glass fibres. Boyle and Smith opened the door to digital cameras by inventing a sensor that turns light into electrical signals. The story of how the two of them worked together on this problem is illuminating, but this short chapter permits me to highlight only one lesson this year's Nobel Prizes for science can teach us in India.

Notice eight of the nine Nobel scientists this year are American citizens; like our own Venki, five of these eight were born in countries other than America; the prizes in chemistry, medicine, and physics are being shared by three scientists each. These facts raise the question, why do the Americans win most of the Nobel prizes?

One reason for their individual success is the team spirit fostered in American culture. Would Dr. Ramakrishnan have won the prize if he were working in India? It is more than likely that several Indian scientists are more brilliant than him. No doubt, they lack the kind of laboratories that are available to Venki... but if you question them (especially if they have worked both in India and in America), they are likely to tell you that more important than material resources, what they miss in our universities is a spirit of cooperation.

A capable microbiologist explained the problem to me: "What wins a Nobel Prize is innovation. But innovation requires questioning existing assumptions, theories, and beliefs. If you appear to be questioning the beliefs of your seniors in the field of *their* specialisation, then you can forget about their support for your projects and grant requests. Our professional culture is such that if your superiors suspect that you might outshine them in a field where they have worked for decades, they will go out of their way to create hurdles for you, just as some of our gods become inauspicious to you simply because you haven't fed their insatiable appetite and ego.

"Our gods are 'omnipresent': They don't remain confined to the temples. They disfigure the culture of our universities as much as they distort our Westminster democracy. The in-house rivalries that have turned into destructive animosities within BJP seem to have taught this bitter lesson to the honourable Arun Shourie. Therefore, each one of the eight senior faculty in his pet project at IIT Kanpur—Biological Sciences and Bioengineering (BSBE)—were recruited abroad, even while Shourie was still proclaiming the nobility of the Hindutva culture. BSBE is hoping that the foreign-trained scientists will bring into our scientific institutions the professional culture of the West. Good and brilliant people like Mr. Shourie are yet to find a way to change the self-destructive culture of our political parties."

The Nobel Peace Prize to President Barack Obama reinforces this significant cultural difference between us and the West. The Norwegian Nobel Committee's decision to award the Peace Prize to his untested 9-month-old presidency has drawn much praise as well as abundant derision and plenty of puzzlement. Right or wrong, the Nobel Prize has raised the bar so high for Obama's presidency that judged in the light of the expectations any failures would be spectacular." And there can be no doubt that many of his ambitious efforts will fail, just like his attempt to bring the Olympics to Chicago. Some plans will fail because no one can control all the outcomes of one's efforts. Other endeavours will fail because of Obama's own ignorance, poor judgement, personal shortcomings, erroneous ideas and beliefs.

It is possible that three years from now the committee will regret its decision. Yet, the question remains: Why did the committee decide to honour President Obama just eleven days after he took office as President of the United States? The committee said that it was for "his extraordinary efforts to strengthen international diplomacy and cooperation between peoples." Even if some of the unexpressed motives behind the award were not so noble, there is certainly merit in the reason given:

Many Muslims see America as their enemy; Iran has described America as the "Great Satan." But President Obama promised to make an effort to love those who hate America, just as he reached out to Hilary Clinton—his one-time arch rival. In offering her the most prominent job in his cabinet, he followed Abraham Lincoln, who had also invited his rivals to help run the government of the then deeply divided USA.

Was Hillary Clinton's appointment political pragmatism? It was...

but seeking to destroy your opponents is also pragmatic politics. Which course you choose depends on the values you cherish. The fact is that Obama is enough of a Christian to value cooperation and love as integral facets of American culture. The Bible says that love is supreme. God is love, and He loves us even when we rebel against Him.

Obama believes that his predecessor, President George W. Bush, was right in going to war against al-Qaeda and the Taliban. But Obama also knows that neither President Bush nor Americans hate Muslims. Even though much of the world cannot comprehend, the fact is that while many Muslim jihadists would love to come to America to kill Americans, any number of individual Americans would gladly spend their life savings to go as volunteers to serve Muslims in Iran, Afghanistan, or Pakistan, knowing perfectly well that they might be kidnapped, raped, or killed.

Why do Americans volunteer to go to Muslim nations to serve? It's because their culture was shaped by a God who sacrificed his life for those who love darkness and hate divine light. I have understood America enough to know that even though President Bush would disagree with some of President Obama's decisions, he would honour and support every effort his successor makes to befriend and serve Muslim nations. If we Indians find it impossible to understand or believe the nobility of this spirit, then that simply shows how our worldview has made us incapable of appreciating, let alone developing a culture that produces Noble Prize- winning scientists and statesmen.

We rarely win a Nobel Prize because supporting and serving our rivals is not part of our culture. Hindu culture was constructed on the idea that some of our neighbours are lower than us and should be kept at a distance. In contrast, American culture was built on the command that people must love their neighbours as themselves and go beyond that to loving their enemies. Have Americans been consistent in obeying the Bible? By no means! Many of them practised slavery, and many continue to practise racism. Capitalistic and academic competition, which is meant to be a competition in excellence, often degenerates into sinful envy, jealousy, meanness, hatred, and destructive rivalries. Nevertheless, their belief that all human beings are made in God's image and therefore have unique dignity has had a powerful impact on their culture. The Bahujan of India remains backward because we find it very hard to cooperate even across jati (caste or sub-caste) boundaries, let alone caste lines, in any way to love and support our neighbours to realise individual, social, or national dreams.

Chapter Twenty-One
The Backwards Can Become Better than the British

Learning a thousand dialects spoken by illiterate Indians in order to turn them into seventy-three literary languages and to create their grammars and dictionaries is a herculean effort at nation building. Why didn't Western missionaries simply teach English so that we may read the Bible in English?

English has already become India's second language. In order to move forward, even Bihar has started pilot projects to teach spoken English to "backward" children. Over 125 million Indians now speak English; that is more than twice as many people as live in Great Britain!

Will English emancipate India's 750 million Bahujans?

Kayasths and Kushwahas are both Shudras, but fifty years ago the Kayasths were classified as 'Forward Castes', while Kachhis, Sainis, and Malis are still "Backward." What made the difference? English education was certainly a central factor. English *can* make India greater than Great Britain. However, for decades OBC leaders such as Manyawar Mulayam Singh Yadav have opposed English, partly because for two hundred years educated, upper-caste Indians have used English as a language not of liberation but of discrimination and elitism. English will *not* move our masses forward unless we allow the spirit of the English language *and* literature to liberate us from attitudes and values deeply embedded in Indian philosophies. Let me explain.

I grew up in the heart of Hindi-stan, in Allahabad, barely two hours from Kashi, where Tulsidas wrote *Ramcharit Manas*. I was always told that my mother tongue came out of his great epic. Therefore, when I started reading the epic, I was puzzled: I couldn't understand a single sentence. His Hindi was very different from mine. That forced me to ask: Where exactly did my mother tongue—our "national" language—come from?

What was the court language in pre-British India?

Hindi and Urdu did not exist as literary languages prior to the British Raj. Muslim scholars had no interest in the language of the thirteenth-century poet Amir Khusro, who had (from their point of view) corrupted their classical languages, Arabic and Persian, by mixing them up with dialects around Delhi. It took the labours of British Bible translator, Rev. Henry Martyn to forge those dialects into a literary language—Urdu. Likewise, even after the Jat rulers of Banaras started promoting Ram Lila in order to organise Hindus against a possible attack by the Nawab of Avadh (Lucknow), learned Brahmins took no interest in developing Tulsidas's khari bol. Annual month-long performances of Ram Lila were the Bollywood of North India at the time. These performances began expanding the geographic reach of khari boli as the common man's dialect. However, khari boli did nothing to enhance the power of the Brahmin priests, and therefore, they were not interested in developing this popular dialect. Therefore, it was left to the missionaries and Bible translators such as Rev. Gilchrist and later Rev. Kellogg, to make Tulsi Das's dialect a base for developing modern Hindi as a literary language.

Was Sanskrit India's court language before the British?

It should have been, but it wasn't. Why? Because, the knowledge of Sanskrit was power, and Brahmins wouldn't share the source of their power even with their own women, let alone with non-Brahmins. Sanskrit is a treasure. Unfortunately, however, those who had the key to this treasure did not love their neighbours enough to want to enrich them. Brahminism made us poor, ignorant, and backward, because the Sanskrit scriptures do not teach that spirituality requires us to "Love your neighbour as yourself." Moral purity, according to our scriptures, required Brahmins to treat their neighbours as untouchables and polluting.

What happened to Ashoka's Pali?

Was Pali the court language of India? Ashoka, the greatest OBC ruler, used the language of the village, "Pali," and the Brahmi script to spread his wisdom and rule throughout India. Pali became the language of Buddhist learning. Yet, at the dawn of the nineteenth century, India did not have even one scholar who could read a sentence inscribed on any one of the Ashoka Pillars found across India. No one had even heard of Ashoka's name until the 1830s, when an Anglo India scholar, James Prinsep—the son of a wealthy MP in England—found the key to reading Brahmi script on Ashoka's pillars.

Ashoka's efforts to unify geographic India by promoting one script, language, and wisdom were magnificent. But why did they fail? Opposition and persecution by Brahmins were factors, but that does not explain why the Brahmi script became extinct. The deeper problem was that Buddhism teaches that the Ultimate Reality is Silence or Shoonya. The human mind is not made in the image of God. It is a product of Avidya (Primeval Ignorance). Therefore, human language, logic, and words can have no correlation with Truth. The way to Enlightenment is through emptying one's mind of all words and thoughts, until one reaches absolute Silence. Thus, Ashoka's religious philosophy worked against his social agenda that could have made India a great, unified nation built by great literature. Buddhist monks barely studied their own scriptures. They had no religious motivation to take the trouble to turn their neighbours' dialects into literary languages in order to make Buddha's thought accessible to everyone. They were teaching techniques to empty one's mind of all thought, not to fill them with great, interesting, or useful ideas.

Language and development

Human beings are the only culture-creating species on this planet. We create culture because we speak. Language is the foundation of creativity and culture; that is why no one can build a great culture without a strong language. A tribe remains stuck in the "Stone Age" until its dialect is enriched by an encounter with a language richer in ideas. We have remained backward because India's religious philosophies conspired against the cultivation of strong national language(s) and literature. When the British Raj began in India, our court language was a foreign one: Persian!

Why would the Mughals use Persian as their court language? Of course, because Jehangir brought Persian soldiers with him; but that does not answer the question. Actually, the Mughals used Persian for the same reason that the Brahmins used Sanskrit instead of Hindi to exclude the rest of us from power. Being Turks, the Moghuls could have used Turkish. But they wanted to exclude even their courtiers from the family discussions. There can be no "government of the people, for the people, and by the people," which operates in a language not understood by the people. Democracy is possible only if the language of the people is the language of government.

Why English reformed England

Up until the sixteenth century, European priests used Latin very much like the Brahmin priests used Sanskrit—to keep the masses in the bondage of ignorance and superstitions. The Bible was available only in Latin, which was the language of learning and courts. Schools and universities belonged to the Church, and the Church's hierarchy used the knowledge of Latin as a means of excluding common people from power. An Oxford reformer, John Wycliffe (1320s–1384), began to challenge this evil. As he studied the Bible, he realised that his Church was doing the very opposite of what God had commanded it to do: to go into the whole world and share the knowledge of truth with every person from every nation group. In Wycliffe's England, scholars spoke in Latin, while various dialects of "English" were spoken by "women and demons.". Wycliffe's vision of reforming England began to be realised at the national level in the 1530s, after William Tyndale succeeded in translating the second part of the Bible (the New Testament) 123 into English. The English establishment opposed his work so much that he had to have it printed in Belgium and smuggled into England. Smuggling scriptures had become necessary because the Church itself had made it illegal to translate the Bible into English. Tyndal paid for his "crime" with his life: he lived as a poor fugitive until he was caught, tried, strangled, and burned in public. The powers understood that by giving the Bible to the masses, Tyndale was demolishing their monopoly over power, religious as well as secular.

Bible translators such as Wycliffe, Luther, and Tyndale reformed Europe because the Bible inspired them to begin the revolution of enriching the dialects of ordinary people with the ideas and vocabulary of classical languages such as Hebrew, Greek, and Latin. These risky literary efforts that challenged the ruling establishment made it possible for the common man's dialects, such as English, to become the language of the church, university, philosophy, science, market, law and the government. Ordinary Europeans were then able to develop their intellectual and spiritual potential and contribute to building great nations.

Can English reform India?

India will not be transformed by doubling or tripling the number of English speakers. Those fortunate enough to study in English medium schools will get jobs, but the vast majority of the Bahujans will remain backward. They will then revolt as the Maoists are attempting in India's Red Corridor.

The British East India Company needed Indian employees who spoke a little English, but it had no interest in educating a class of Indians who would enrich Indian vernaculars, educate the masses, and prepare India for liberty and self-government. That was the agenda of the missionaries who came to India because they obeyed Jesus' command to love their neighbours as themselves. One only needs to read Charles Grant (1792), Raja Ram Mohan Roy (1823),

Alexander Duff (1830), Charles Trevelyan (1834 & 38), and his brother-in-law, Lord Macaulay (1833 & 35), to realise that they had to oppose the classicists who wanted to promote Sanskrit, Arabic, and Persian, in order to choose English as the means of enriching our vernaculars. Their goal was to empower India's masses.

Critics such as Arun Shourie have neither read nor understood people such as Ram Mohan Roy and Lord Macaulay. Mahatma Gandhi (a British-educated Gujarati) and Rabindranath Tagore (a Bengali-speaking scholar of English) understood Macaulay. The two of them met together in the 1920s and reached the conclusion that Hindi had to be India's future—not Sanskrit and not English. But Hindi will not develop our masses unless the educated, English-speaking Indians love their backward neighbours enough to enrich the vernaculars. This is why *FORWARD* Press magazine, which published these chapters as monthly articles, has chosen to be fully bilingual. The magazine is using English and Hindi to enrich each other.

Why did missionary reformers develop vernaculars?

A few years ago, a Malayalee scholar from Mumbai, Dr. Babu Verghese, submitted a 700-page PhD thesis to the University of Nagpur. It demonstrated that seventy-three modern Indian literary languages were created by Bible translators using the dialects of mostly illiterate Indians. These include the national languages of India (Hindi), Pakistan (Urdu), and Bangladesh (Bengali). Five Brahmin scholars examined Dr. Verghese's thesis and awarded him a Ph.D. The examiners went on to record a unanimous recommendation that his thesis, when published as a book, should be required reading for students of Indian linguistics.

Learning a thousand dialects spoken by illiterate Indians in order to turn them into seventy-three literary languages and to create their grammars and dictionaries is a herculean effort at nation building. Why didn't Western missionaries simply teach English so that we may read the Bible in English?

Three English missionaries—William Carey, Joshua Marshman,

and William Ward—began this gigantic mission to create modern India, in the year 1800, on the banks of the river Hooghly, in Serampore (Srirampur), near Calcutta. In 1818, the trio also founded a college, which became Serampore University. They chose to use Bengali, rather than English, as the medium of instruction in their college. Why? Because the missionaries noticed that Indian families wanted their children to learn enough English to get a job with the East India Company. The "job," however, brought their real learning and service to their communities to a quick and permanent end. The missionaries had not dedicated their lives to produce good English-speaking servants for the British Raj! They wanted Indians to come to their college to begin cultivating their minds and their spirits, to question the socio-economic darkness around them, to inquire and find truth, which is what liberates individuals and builds great nations. The Bible teaches that the Creator gave us the gift of language because He loves us. Love includes communication, and communication of great ideas requires great language.

What is love? India has remained backward because our religiosity produced caste and untouchability—the antithesis of love. While the English language can get us jobs, ideas in English literature can help us understand love that can transform India—the kind of love that drove men and women who gave us our modern languages. Therefore, in the next chapter, let us look at love in Shakespeare's play *Romeo and Juliet*.

Chapter Twenty-two
Needed: More Romeos

At the end of the play, Romeo and Juliet seal their love with their blood... their love and sacrifice reconcile their families.

Many Indians think that Shakespeare's Romeo is like Laila-Majnu, driven crazy by erotic love that the Greeks called *Eros*. The reality is that Shakespeare wrote his play *Romeo and Juliet* in England at a time when the two major Christian groups, Protestants and Catholics, hated each other enough to prevent their children from marrying each other, just like the play's two warring households in the Italian city of Verona. Juliet enabled Romeo to transform sexual infatuation into Christ-like love (agape) for her and her household (caste). Their love made it possible for them to lay down their lives for each other and to reconcile their warring "castes." Shakespeare states the point of his play in the opening lines:

> Two households, both alike in dignity,
> In fair Verona, where we lay our scene,
> From ancient grudge break to new mutiny,
> Where civil blood makes civil hands unclean.
> From forth the fatal loins of these two foes
> A pair of star-cross'd lovers take their life;
> Whose misadventured piteous overthrows
> Do with their death bury their parents' strife.

The previous chapter suggested that we are "backward," in part, because no Hindu, Buddhist, or Muslim scholar, religious leader, or king loved us enough to make sustained effort to develop our vernaculars. Our religious cultures conspired to ensure that classical languages—Sanskrit, Arabic, and Persian—would be used to exclude us from power that comes from knowledge.

During the British era, reformers such as Raja Ram Mohan Roy and rulers such as Lord Macaulay felt that the English language could enrich India's vernaculars. However, the upper castes who learned English used it to advance their own interests, rather than the interests of the common people. Will the Bahujan "creamy layer" do exactly what every other creamy layer does? That is, create a gulf that separates the rich from the poor, and the powerful from the rest?

India desperately needs the spirituality that enabled Romeo to love his enemies—that is, Juliet's family. That force was a peculiar kind of love promoted by the classics of English literature and the source of that literature—the Bible.

When the Government of Tamil Nadu began erecting along the beautiful Marina Beach in Chennai the statues of the creators of modern Tamil, it honoured three Christian missionaries: Italian Jesuit Constanzo Beschi, English Missionaries Bishop Robert Caldwell and Dr. G. U. Pope, and only one Brahmin, Mahakavi Subramanya Bharathi, who renounced his Brahmin identity—just as Romeo renounced his Montague identity—in order to love those considered enemies by his caste. An important question is: Why didn't English missionaries just teach us English? Why did they take the trouble to develop our languages?

Was it just to convert us? If so, wouldn't the objective of conversion have been served better had they taught our leaders English, hired them in their businesses and institutions, and made promotions conditional on conversions? Why did they not do that?

Unless we study the Bible and the literature that it shaped, we cannot understand the Agape (divine) love that drove Christian missionaries to serve us, including studying our dialects in order to turn them into literary languages. As mentioned earlier, their labours made it possible for Hindi, Urdu, and Bengali to become, popularly speaking, national languages of India, Pakistan, and Bangladesh. Unless the language of the people is made the language of learning and governing, it is not possible to have a "government of the people, for the people, and by the people." Our own religious scholars did not love us enough to take the trouble to cultivate our dialects. It is a difficult labour, especially if the beneficiaries cannot even pay the scholars to give them the language that they need to develop.

William Tyndale, who translated and published the first Bible (New Testament) into English, deeply offended the ruling elite. He was taking the very source of their power—knowledge—and giving it to the common man. The rulers convicted him and strangled and burned him at the stake. Yet Tyndale's labour created modern English and reformed his nation, including by producing writers like Shakespeare. These writers were nurtured in Tyndale's language, and in the Bible, which was incorporated into the Geneva Bible before Shakespeare, and into the King James Bible soon after Shakespeare retired from the Globe Theatre.

English-speaking missionaries came to India to do for us what our own socio-religious leaders did not do, because the Bible taught them that God is love and that the divine love gives itself sacrificially without conditions and without expectation of reward, simply because that is God's nature, and only to accomplish good for us. The Bible's most famous verse is John 3:16, "For God so loved the world that He gave His only begotten Son that whosoever believes in Him should not perish but have everlasting life." Jesus demonstrated God's love not simply by serving the poor and the sick who were victims of the beastly kingdoms of this world but supremely by sacrificing his own life to reconcile God's enemies—sinners—with God, and human enemies with each other: the Jews with non-Jewish Gentiles, Greeks and Barbarians, slaves and free, upper castes and lower castes. In Shakespeare's hands, Romeo's love for Juliet grows to become like Christ's love for us.

Romeo's spiritual transformation happens in the famous Balcony Scene, when Juliet says to him that he cannot marry her unless he forsakes his name, that is, his family identity. Nothing else but their names separated them from each other, because their family identities had become inextricably intertwined with hatred for the other family. Romeo agreed that his family was defined and controlled by hatred for Juliet's family and, therefore, his name (the object of her family's hatred) would never allow him to marry into her family.

If you study the Bible, you will understand that Juliet asked Romeo to do exactly what the Lord Jesus had asked his Jewish disciples to do. They despised non-Jews as untouchables, just as Romeo's family detested Juliet's family. Jesus shocked them when he said, anyone who wants to follow me into the kingdom of heaven, must hate his father and mother, his wife and children, his brothers and sisters—yes, even his own life" (Luke 14:26). Here, "hate" means to *set aside*. If Romeo married Juliet, his family would conclude that he hates his father and mother, brothers and cousins, simply because he does not hate what they hate. In fact, he loves whom they hate. Romeo's transformation required him to set aside his family's identity that was inextricably intertwined with hatred for her family. How do we know that Romeo's transformation was spiritual? His inner spiritual change becomes visible when, (like Jesus Christ) he bears the undeserved insult and abuse of Juliet's cousin without retaliating. Juliet's love for Romeo also renounces her family's hatred for Romeo's family. For a while, that step appears to be hating her own family.

Shakespeare, a Protestant, portrays Friar Laurence, a Roman Catholic, as a good and wise Christian priest. He agrees to marry Romeo and Juliet, risking the wrath of both the families. Why? He marries them precisely because he sees that their love could bring their families' mutual hatred to an end. The priest says,

> In one respect I'll thy assistant be;
>
> For this alliance may so happy prove,
>
> To turn your households' rancour to pure love.

At the end of the play, Romeo and Juliet seal their love with their blood. Thanks to the priest and the Prince of Verona, their love and sacrifice reconcile their families. Juliet's father, Capulet, calls Romeo's father "brother", and asks for his hand of friendship. Romeo's father replies that he would build a statue of pure gold for "true and faithful Juliet." Juliet's father acknowledges that their death was a sacrifice to end "our enmity."

Since the caste system has made the Bahujans "backward," knowledge of the English language is not sufficient to move our people forward. We have to demolish the caste system itself. How can that be done?

In America, it took a civil war under the leadership of Abraham Lincoln to end slavery. Not many Indians know that the majority of the Americans who died fighting against slavery were white, not black. That is why Mahatma Jotiba Phule dedicated his book *Slavery* to Americans. But why did white Christians fight against fellow whites to liberate the blacks? When Abraham Lincoln first met Mrs. Harriet Beecher Stowe, he exclaimed, "So, you are that little lady who wrote the book that started this big war!" What did she write? For decades, along with great preachers such as Charles Finney, Harriet's father and brothers had expounded the Bible's teachings against slavery. Harriet turned biblical preaching into a powerful piece of literature, *Uncle Tom's Cabin*. Her story moved millions of white Americans against slavery because they understood why the Lord Jesus taught that to love God meant to love our neighbours as ourselves—not to enslave them or to despise them as lower class or untouchables.

Devout Christians in America had to wage a civil war to end slavery, but the British were able to end their slave trade without a war through a democratic struggle led by Christian politicians such as William Wilberforce. Wilberforce succeeded only because his anti-slavery movement was built upon the religious revivals of preachers such as John Wesley, who wrote, *Thoughts on Slavery*, describing slavery as "the execrable sum of human villainy."

Christian philosopher John Locke called slavery "so vile and miserable an estate of man, and so directly opposite to the generous temper and courage of our nation, that it is hardly to be conceived that an Englishman, much less a gentleman, should plead for it..." In *Wealth of Nations*, Christian thinker Adam Smith exposed slavery as economically inefficient. Aphra Behn wrote the first novel,

Oroonoko, or *The History of the Royal Slave*, in which the hero was a slave. Wilberforce and his fellow Abolitionists widely distributed William Cowper's *The Negro's Complaint*, in which Cowper carried his Abolitionist passions into poetry. It is important to understand that this literary and political campaign succeeded only because it was undergirded by the Bible, which the British culture knew was the Word of God. In order to improve the morals of his nation, Wilberforce championed the Bible Society.

The Bible also inspired Indian writers such as Rabindranath Tagore to write against caste and untouchability. His dance-drama *Chandalika* is based on Jesus' encounter with an untouchable woman described in the fourth chapter of the Gospel of John. Even though Tagore's work is powerful, it had little impact in turning the upper castes against untouchability because he replaced a historical fact (of Jesus meeting a Samaritan woman) with an imaginary Buddhist monk who meets Chandalika at the well. Fiction carries little authority when it is separated from truth. Romeo and Juliet is fiction. It became Shakespeare's most popular play only because it expounded the Bible's view of true, divine love.

Today, people who do not read the Bible, and therefore do not understand Shakespeare, might dismiss this chapter, insisting that *Romeo and Juliet* is about nothing more than sensual love. Even if one argues that the play describes only erotic love, the fact remains that we need to read Shakespeare in order to learn the right orientation of sexual love from the Bible rather than from Gandhi, Krishna, Ram, or the Buddha.

Romeo gave his life for his wife; while the Buddha deserted his wife in search of his own enlightenment. Gandhi gave up sexual relations with his wife but "experimented" with many women in his ashrams. How can our culture treat an adulterer as a mahatma (a great soul)? We are able to do so because our icon of sexual love, Krishna, had 16,000 wives, yet none of them is worshipped. His mistress is! That is why our people are able to elect politician's mistresses as chief ministers. Ram loved his wife, Sita, enough to wage a war to win her back from Ravan. But unlike Romeo, he loved his honour much more than his wife. The fire god testified that Sita was pure, yet Ram sent her into exile because his reputation was more important to him than his wife.

Today, the sun is setting in the West... Western families are falling apart, because the West has turned its back on its own spiritual and literary heritage. After adopting our Bhagwans, such as Rajneesh, the West is espousing the spirituality of Khajuraho and Tantra.

That is why it might be possible for "backward castes" to become even better than the British. But that will not happen through the English language alone: We need to learn erotic as well as divine love from Shakespeare and the Bible—a love that will build strong men, women, and children, and therefore strong families, which is what creates a strong nation.

PART VII

THE CURE

Chapter Twenty-Three
The Secret of Obama's Victory

Americans did not always practise what they believed, because they are also sinners. The difference between India and America is that while our culture believes that inequality is the truth, American culture says that the truth is that all human beings are created equal.

Some atheists asked the American Supreme Court to prevent President Obama from invoking God while taking his oath of office on 20 January 2009. The Court ignored their plea. Obama humbled himself before God publicly and put his hand on his hero Abraham Lincoln's Bible to take his oath. As an Indian, I was so intrigued that I made ten videos on this topic. (See www. YouTube.com/ VishalMangalwadi1)

Atheists think that they are smart, but President Obama knows that without the Bible he could not have won the presidency, and without God, the minorities (such as blacks or Indians) cannot be safe in America.

Democracy depends upon majority votes; and since "whites" are still the majority in America, why should they grant equal rights to the minorities, let alone elect someone from a minority community to rule over them? Even before Obama, a Democrat, was elected president, the highly conservative southern state of Louisiana elected Bobby Jindal as their governor.

Atheists will tell you that they believe in human equality but not in God or the Bible. But ask them, "Why do you believe that all human beings are equal?" and they will answer: "Equality is self-evident." For that matter, the American Declaration of Independence states; "We hold these truths to be self-evident—that all men are created equal.

"Not to me," I respond. My ancestors were not stupid. They observed human beings carefully and saw that everyone was unequal. The observable fact of human inequality raised the question: Why are people born unequal? Our sages explained self-evident inequality in two ways: (a) God created people unequal, and (b) Souls are born high or low, male or female, because of their good or bad karma.

I ask atheists: "Have blacks or women experienced themselves as equal in America?" The honest ones always say, "No."

"If equality is not self-evident, then why do you believe in human equality?"

"Well..." they fumble a bit before thinking out loud... "everyone must have *evolved* equal by chance."

That gives away the naivety of atheism. Evolution is a theory to explain *inequality*—why some animals are superior to others. How can anyone build a credible case for equality on the basis of a theory invented to explain inequality?

President Obama knows that Americans believed that blacks and whites, men and women, were equal because the Bible says that

> (a) All human beings are created in God's image;
>
> (b) All people alive today have descended from one set of parents—Adam and Eve. Blacks and whites did not evolve from different sets of monkeys;
>
> (c) The Bible's teaching on sin also implies equality. A Shudra is a sinner, so is a Brahmin. Therefore, both are separated from God. A Brahmin is not closer to God just because he was born into a Brahmin family, but
>
> (d) The Bible goes on to indicate that we are also equal because God loves us all equally, and sent Jesus to save all of us from our sins;
>
> (e) It was the German reformer Martin Luther's discovery of the Bible's teaching of "priesthood of all believers" that began the modern movement for equality. This doctrine means that every

Shudra who has repented of his/her sins and has been "born-again to become a child of God's love is already a holy priest, just as every Brahmin can become a genuine priest by renouncing Brahminism's sin of untouchability and believing the truth.

Of course, Americans did not always practise what they believed, because they were also sinners. The difference between India and America is that while our culture believes that inequality is the truth, American culture says that the truth is that all human beings are created equal. Therefore, in American culture, it is sin not to love our neighbours as ourselves. In contrast, our sages said that it was sin to socialise with some of our neighbours.

Even though Americans have not always practised truth yet, as Jesus said, the truth liberates. Affirming the truth of human equality enabled Abraham Lincoln to win the war against slavery. It helped Martin Luther King Jr. win the battle for equal civil rights for blacks. And it helped President Obama win the presidency.

Obama couldn't have won without the vote of Hillary Clinton's supporters. Why did she support him after losing to him in a bitter primary campaign? That's not how it is in India or many other countries. We have over nine hundred political parties, and not one of them can hold democratic primaries. The losing candidate would sabotage the winner's chances in the main election. Indian politicians are driven by the "will to power," as the philosopher Nietzsche said that people in a godless universe would be.

But Hillary Clinton was driven by something more than this. Listen to what she said at the Democratic National Convention in Denver:

"I ran for president to renew the promise of America. ... to fight for an America defined by deep and meaningful equality. To help every child live up to his or her God-given potential... [to] make our government an instrument of the public good, not of private plunder... Those are the reasons I ran for president. Those are the reasons I support Barack Obama. And those are the reasons you should too."

If Clinton were an Indian politician, she would have ensured that

Obama lost. But instead, she put her personal feelings and ambitions aside and supported Obama.

By doing this, she was drawing on her biblical roots. But even if she wasn't convinced personally, she had to do this because the Bible has historically set the standards Americans expect from their leaders. American politicians have to submit their ambitions to moral principles. They have to put "public good" over "private plunder," as Clinton put it. It allows Clinton to endorse the man who defeated her, and Obama to invite his most dangerous rival to serve as his most important teammate.

Chapter Twenty-four
Moving Forward—Korean Style

It was the miraculous historical example of Moses that inspired Kim Yong-Ki to believe that God could also deliver his people from Japan's tyranny and transform their useless land into a Canaan, a productive land flowing with milk and honey.

In 2012, a small farmer in Yong Am village was already earning Rs 28 lakh (approximately $62,000) per year, and they were making plans to increase this to Rs 45 lakh per year by 2015! Today it is one of the richest villages in Korea. But just thirty years ago, it was one of the poorest; hidden in a mountain and covered by snow for more than three months in a year, without a single road, running water, or electricity. Back then, there were no jobs; everyone was dependent on subsistence agriculture. There was no organised school, politics, or religion; they worshipped the spirits of their own ancestors and tree spirits. Occasionally they went to the Buddhist temple on the mountain, but the priests were seeking their own nirvana from this world of suffering. Therefore, they made no effort to organise the community in any way or to teach anyone anything of practical, worldly value.

In their ability and ingenuity, the Buddhist monks were second to none. To them belongs the credit for bringing literacy to Korea. Their art, sculptures, and architecture are superb. Their unique glory lies in the fact that they invented moveable metal fonts and began printing at least two centuries before the Europeans. Unfortunately, however, the scriptures they printed did not inspire anyone with a hope and a vision for building a great Korea. Consequently, in a generation or two ago, in villages such as Yong Am, practically everyone was illiterate and uneducated, at least in the modern sense of the term. The village was also divided socially, in a milder version of India's own caste system. A man was considered wealthy if he could afford to "own" more than one wife. Women were second class creatures, and children were not groomed to seek a future better than their parents.

Yong Am village has sixty-three families; of these, just over half own about two hectares each, the rest own less, if any, agricultural land. Thirty years ago, they grew corn, potatoes, and sweet potatoes—but not enough to sell. They lived at subsistence level because they could not preserve potatoes even for their own consumption. There was no cold storage. Now all that has changed. They have organised themselves into an agricultural industry. All the families farm together without caste distinctions. They grow flowers and export them to Japan. They sell a medicinal plant, Shinsuncho, to companies that make health drinks. They grow fruit and dry it for the whole year. Even before electricity arrived in the village, a technique had been developed to preserve potatoes in specially designed caves in the mountains.

Now, exporters and food-processing companies are able to sign yearly contracts with the farmers, insurance companies are eager to insure the crops, and banks are more than willing to give loans for agricultural development, because these small farmers have organised themselves together to follow strict codes of agribusiness ethics and rigorous rules of quality control. They orchestrate the timing of their production and harvesting, not according to seasons, but to meet the market's tastes and demands. They supply fresh flowers when both Japan and Korea are covered with snow!

Isn't agriculture dependent on seasons?

Not in Yong Am. Most of them no longer worship nature or its governing spirits. They are establishing their own authority over nature, because they have begun to believe that they were created in the image of their Creator in order to establish their dominion over nature. In line with this new belief, much of the cultivation now happens in greenhouses, where freezing temperatures outside make no difference to the crops inside. In fact, sensitive crops are grown in greenhouses made of two layers of heavy plastic. During the winter months, the top layer is covered with snow, but water is circulated between the two layers at 10 degrees Celsius. That keeps the inside temperature warm enough to grow whenever the crops are wanted by the buyers. The water is not supplied by a public dam built by the government. Farmers pump it up from below the ground. In fact, the farmers pay a tax to the government to use the water under their own lands.

What transformed Yong Am?

Thirty-eight years ago, an unusual farmer, Kim Yong Ki, bought fifty hectares of mountainous wasteland just outside of Yong Am village. Since no one wanted to buy this useless wilderness, he was able to get it at a price equivalent to one cigarette packet per pyong—the smallest unit of land that is sold in Korea. In fact, Kim Yong-Ki bought the land precisely because it was unproductive wilderness. He wanted it to be a model, so he called his farm Canaan. That is the original name for the land now called Israel. Kim chose that name because his vision to transform his nation was inspired by the Bible's narrative concerning Canaan—a prosperous land "flowing with milk and honey."

About 3,500 years ago, the Israelites or Jews were called Hebrews. They were slaves in Egypt. When Egyptian slave masters became especially cruel, the Hebrews cried out to God, who sent Moses to deliver them from their slavery. Moses was not meditating when he "met" God. He was grazing his sheep on a mountain and saw a bush burning. He became curious when the bush kept burning on and on. He went to figure out why it was not burnt out, and was startled when a voice came from the bush asking him to take off his shoes because it was sacred ground. The voice claimed to be that of the God of his forefathers Abraham, Isaac, and Jacob; that He had seen the misery of His people, heard their cries; and had come to deliver them from their slavery. God said that He would take them out of their slavery into a land He had promised their fathers, a land of liberty and prosperity—the land of Canaan. God asked Moses to go to Pharaoh and give His message: Let *My* people go, so that they may serve Me (instead of you)!

Moses could not believe the voice. Nor was he eager to undertake such a suicidal mission. The second book of the Bible, called Exodus, describes how sceptical Moses was about whether the voice was, in fact, God's (Chapter 3). To cut the long story short: Moses became instrumental in transforming slaves into owners and rulers of Canaan. That amazing transformation is recorded in the first five books of the Bible. It was that miraculous historical event that inspired Kim Yong-Ki to believe that God could also deliver his people from Japan's tyranny and transform their useless land into a Canaan.

Kim is actually his surname, like Chaturvedi. The story of his own transformation begins with his mother, Kim Kang Yun. Although she was a simple, poor peasant, thanks to her high-class Buddhist background, she was literate. Like everyone else, her family was experiencing the awful impact of Japan's tyrannical rule. One day, while she was working on her farm, a Western missionary passed by and dropped a pamphlet. It explained this verse from the Bible: "For God so loved the world that He gave His only begotten son, so that whosoever believes in Him should not perish but have everlasting life" (John 3:16). The spirits that Kang Yun worshipped demanded all sorts of sacrifices from her but never did anything to save her from her misery. So, she was intrigued to read about a God who sacrificed for her. She knew that she loved her baby enough to sacrifice herself for him. Therefore, it made sense to her that her Creator might love her enough to make a sacrifice to save her. She had been taught that one had to work hard over many lifetimes to save oneself. So, the information that God could save her in this life appealed to her. She decided to learn more about her Creator, and in order to serve the Creator, she only decided to discard all lesser deities. Her husband, who was well read in Chinese Buddhist literature, agreed with her reasoning. They decided to send their son to Kwang Dong Secondary School, run by Yeo Woon Young, a devout scholar who influenced many leaders of modern Korea.

Yeo Woon Young taught Kim to study the Bible. And the Bible taught Kim that God is not a "meditator", who dreams up this world. God is a worker. He worked to create the world. Therefore, we cannot be godly if we do not *work* diligently. The Bible also taught Kim that God does not want his children to be poor, living in slums. He put Adam and Eve in a garden because He wanted to bless His children with abundant life. Kim accepted the Bible's teaching that poverty is a result of human sin, which brought curse upon the earth. Our sinfulness has made life difficult, but God is ready to forgive our sins. He sent Jesus to save us from our sin and its consequences, such as slavery, tyranny, and poverty.

Kim realised that God wanted him to love his neighbours as himself, therefore, *service* became as important for him as *work*.

Sacrifice was the third important lesson that Kim learned from Jesus. His life's mission was shaped by Jesus' teaching, "Seek first His [God's] kingdom and His righteousness, and all these things (like food, clothing, and shelter) will be given to you as well" (Matthew 6:33).

Such teachings made Kim a man who prayed as hard as he worked. He believed God and began to buy wastelands, using diligent work and creativity to turn them into model farms. Christ's spirit of service and sacrifice began to manifest itself in his efforts to help his neighbours benefit from his own experiments, creative innovations, and work-habits. He soon realised that Korea could not be transformed by innovations and projects alone. It was even more important to change his people's traditional mindset and cultural values. Therefore, he became as passionate about teaching true godliness as about good agriculture.

His first community, Bongdan Ideal Village (1931–1945), was established during the Japanese occupation. His faith in God gave him such fearlessness that he made it a centre for cultivating nationalism along with sweet potatoes. He began inspiring his people to seek political and economic freedom. That is why he is sometimes called the Korean Gandhi.

On 9 March 1962, the then President of South Korea, Park Chung-hee, visited Dr. Kim's fourth home and farm in Hwangsan Canaan Farm. What he saw so inspired him that he said, "This home and this farm have carried out a revolution in advance of our nation. If all our people were like this, the backwardness of our country would rapidly disappear." The Government of Korea began sending officials to study in Canaan Farmers School in order to nationalise his effort through the New Village Movement (Saemaeul Undong). That grassroots movement began transforming Korea into a modern economic powerhouse that is now blessing many poor countries.

Canaan Farm is now led by his equally visionary and hardworking son, Dr. Kim Bum-il. Under his leadership, the movement began impacting the world. In 1991, he established the first Canaan farm outside Korea, in Bangladesh. In 2006, he visited India and was recognized by the then president, Dr. Abdul Kalam, as a model that India needed. In India, Bihar is the first state where Canaan has begun training grassroots leaders. The number of leaders who have been trained by Canaan Farmers School in Korea and around the world exceeds seven lakh.

Since 2007, their most effective training happens in Canaan Global Leadership Center, which runs a 3-month-long school in partnership with Yonsei University in Seoul, South Korea. Proven world leaders such as Randall Hoag teach community leaders of developing nations subjects such as:

1. Pioneering Mindset
2. Project Management
3. Leadership Skills
4. Organic Agriculture
5. Community Development
6. Economic Development
7. Environmental Management
8. Global Governance and Civil Society
9. Public Health
10. Computer Skills

The good news is that some Koreans, inspired by Dr. Kim, have dedicated their lives to bring these nation-building ideas, values, attitudes, skills, and projects to the poorest parts of India.

Chapter Twenty-five
Republic Day's Magic
A Key to Ending Our Backwardness

The Constitution adopted on 26 January 1950 implied a decision that, from that day, we would do what Moses had commanded Israel to do—become a people governed by law, not men.

Two of Hollywood's greatest minds, Steven Spielberg and George Lucas, teamed up in 1981 to make a super hit movie, *Raiders of the Lost Ark*. The film is set during World War II. German Nazis are searching for the gold-covered, wooden Ark (or chest) that Israel's liberator, Moses, had made approximately 3,400 years ago. The Nazis believe that the Ark's magic will make their armies invincible. The headquarters of the American army, Pentagon, begins to panic. So, it hires an archaeologist, played by Harrison Ford, to find the Ark before the Nazis do. He finds it—and that is what launches the *Indiana Jones* franchise.

The historical Ark did indeed contain the secret of ancient Israel's greatness. That same secret made modern Europe and America the greatest civilizations in history. On 26 January 1950, India adopted that magic as its own. That is what we celebrate as Republic Day. Understanding and internalising that magic could help end our backwardness. The secret is: National greatness lies in pursuing wisdom more than power. Let's recount the meaning and history of our Republic Day before decoding the Ark's mystery.

For thousands of years, we Indians were ruled by men. Twenty-sixth January 1950 became a historic moment when, "we, the people" of India, gave to ourselves, a Constitution that made us into a sovereign republic. Its preamble read,

WE, THE PEOPLE OF India, having solemnly resolved to

constitute India into a SOVEREIGN DEMOCRATIC REPUBLIC and to secure to all citizens:

JUSTICE, social, economic and political;

LIBERTY of thought, expression, belief, faith, and worship; EQUALITY of status and of opportunity, and to promote among them all;

FRATERNITY assuring the dignity of the individual and the unity of the Nation;

IN OUR CONSTITUENT ASSEMBLY this twenty-sixth day of November, 1949, DO HEREBY ADOPT, ENACT AND GIVE TO OURSELVES THIS CONSTITUTION.

The Constitution implied that we decided, from that day, to do what Moses had commanded Israel to do—become a people governed by law, not men. We decided that our leaders would be servants of the law. We would elect them in accordance with the law. They would govern in accordance with the law. We would keep them accountable as per the law. And they would make sure that we, the people, abide by the law.

The first meeting of the Constituent Assembly of India was held in Delhi on 9 December 1946, when the British were still ruling undivided India. The idea of this assembly had come out of negotiations between Indian leaders and the members of the British Cabinet Mission. The assembly was elected by the members of the provincial legislative assemblies. These assemblies, in turn, had been elected under the India Act of 1935. That act, written by the British Raj, served as the Constitution of India at that time. Eventually it became the basis for our new Constitution.

The Constituent Assembly elected Dr. Rajendra Prasad as its president as well as the President of the Interim Government of India. It worked through at least seventeen different committees, whose recommendations were fed to the Drafting Committee headed by Dr. Bhimrao Ambedkar. On 26 November 1949, the assembly approved the constitution presented by the drafting committee, and on 26 January 1950, it replaced the India Act of

1935. At that point, the Constituent Assembly became the Provisional Parliament of India and continued serving until 1952, when the first elections were held under the new Constitution.

Several tributaries had come together to form The India Act of 1935. The first was The Government of India Act of 1919, enacted by the British Parliament. Its preamble expressed the British commitment, which was "...the gradual development of self-governing institutions, with a view to the progressive realisation of responsible government in India as an integral part of the British Empire." Some Indian leaders liked the act, but the Indian National Congress expressed strong disappointment.

Therefore, Mrs. Annie Besant and some of her Indian friends began the second stream that contributed to the Constitution. They started an unofficial effort to draft a new constitution for India. Their vision was revised and approved by an all-party convention held at Kanpur in April 1925. Mr. George Lansbury redrafted it as a statute and introduced it in the House of Commons on 9 December 1925, under the title, "The Commonwealth of India Bill." The Bill sought to make India a dominion of the British Commonwealth like Canada or New Zealand. It included a Bill of Rights, guaranteeing personal liberty, freedom of conscience, freedom of speech, and equality of sexes. The proposal, however, did not arouse any popular enthusiasm because it was for India but not by Indians. Also, at that stage, India's nationalist movement was more interested in opposing the existing system rather than proposing how India should be governed.

The negative stance of Indian leaders, including Mahatma Gandhi, was most vividly expressed in their opposition to the Simon Commission. Gandhi's proven ability to oppose prompted the Secretary of State for India, Lord Birkenhead, to challenge Indian leaders to propose a constitution for India. He implied that India was so complex and our leaders were so incompetent that they could not possibly come up with a proposal that would be accepted by the various Indian communities, including princely states.

The leaders of several parties took up his challenge and

constituted a committee under the chairmanship of Motilal Nehru. His son, Jawaharlal, served as the secretary to this committee. It submitted the "Nehru Report" of 1928 as a Memorandum to the British Government. The report accepted dominion status for India within the British Commonwealth. However, as British leaders had thought, the Nehru Report succeeded only in uniting various Muslim groups as one powerful political force. Mohammad Ali Jinnah went beyond rejecting the report. He offered his famous Fourteen Points that could have kept Pakistan within the Indian Union. Ultimately, India was partitioned because the Congress could not accommodate his concerns, which were accepted by most groups of Muslims.

Nevertheless, along with the Simon Commission's report, the Nehru Report served as a basis for discussions at the Round Table Conferences during 1930–32. These resulted in the India Act of 1935, the basis for our present Constitution. The Constitution, that is, the law of the land, is an idea or an intellectual force that has been transforming India for six decades. Why is it important to remember this history?

We can only imagine what India would be, had we beaten the British in 1857. The most likely scenario is that in 1858 India would have become hundreds of feudal states at war against each other. That would have tempted a Maratha, Jat, or Muslim ruler to unite our warring princely states to start another empire. We would still be ruled by men, not by law.

The British gave us the notion of the rule of law, but they did not invent it. They learned it from ancient Israel. This powerful idea began five hundred years before Moses. We read about it in Chapter 18 of Genesis, the first book of the Bible. Just before cities called Sodom and Gomorrah were to be destroyed because of their wickedness, God said to Abraham that in contrast to these cities, he would become a great and mighty nation because he would teach his children and his household after him, to walk in God's ways and follow righteousness and justice.

Abraham's great-grandchildren became unjust and sold their

brother Joseph into slavery. Little did they realise that they were, in fact, condemning their own descendants to four hundred years of slavery in Egypt! This is similar to what happened in India; by enslaving Shudras, Brahminism divided and weakened India, condemning the whole nation to slavery and colonialism for a thousand years.

Exodus, the second book of the Bible, tells the story of Moses and the Israelites' miraculous deliverance from slavery. But there was a greater challenge before Moses, which was exactly the same as faced by our leaders such as Pandit Jawaharlal Nehru and Dr. Ambedkar. How to transform a bunch of slaves into a mighty nation? Moses followed the recipe that God had given to his ancestor, Abraham. Moses took God's law—the Ten Commandments—and put them in the Ark of the Covenant. He put that chest into the very heart of the nation—into the holiest place in a mobile temple or tabernacle. In the book of Deuteronomy, Moses taught the Israelites that they would become a great nation if they made copies of God's law, wrote it on their doors, and taught it to their children. They would retain their freedom and become prosperous if they and their rulers meditated on God's law, day and night, and did not turn from it to the left or to the right. On the other hand, if they refused to live by God's law, they would condemn themselves again to be ruled by sinful men.

After the nation of Israel settled into what is now the land of Israel, their most famous king, David, built a new tabernacle and brought Moses' Ark into it. His son, Solomon, built a magnificent temple in Jerusalem and, once again, put the law of God into the very heart of the nation. David and Solomon established a tradition of temple-worship and singing that cultivated a unique culture of justice and righteousness. Our religiosity did no such thing for us. The songs the Jews sang taught their children to internalise God's law. These songs are found in the book of Psalms in the middle of the Bible. Here is the very first Psalm:

> 1 Blessed is the one who does not walk in step with the wicked
> or stand in the way that sinners take or sit in the company of

mockers,

> 2 but whose delight is in the law of the LORD, and who meditates on his law, day and night.

> 3 That person is like a tree planted by streams of water, which yields its fruit in season and whose leaf does not wither—whatever they do prospers.

> 4 Not so the wicked! They are like chaff that the wind blows away.

> 5 Therefore the wicked will not stand in the judgement, nor sinners in the assembly of the righteous.

> 6 For the LORD watches over the way of the righteous, but the way of the wicked leads to destruction.

Songs such as this one established the principle of rule of law in the hearts of the people of Israel. They ensured that God's law became the light by which people lived. When they lived by righteous law, they indeed prospered. When they became corrupt and wicked, they destroyed themselves and their nation. To honour the moral law is not the same as to live by it. The Jews' inability to live by God's law taught them that sin is so much a part of our human nature that in our own strength we are incapable of keeping God's law. Therefore, their prophets, such as Isaiah, Jeremiah, and Ezekiel, prophesied that God would send a Saviour who would save them from their sin. He would give them a new spiritual birth. As a result, the law of God, that had been engraved on the tablets of stone, would be written in their hearts. These prophecies were fulfilled by the Lord Jesus Christ, who came to save the world from sin, which is what makes a mockery of righteous law. Jesus began transforming people's hearts by giving them God's own Holy Spirit.

Our Constitution has exerted the kind of powerful reforming influence that Mosaic Law did in Israel. However, Dr. Ambedkar knew perfectly well that the Constitution that his committee gave to India reflected ideals that were way above the actual reality of Indian society. And at the end of the day, our Constitution condemns us as much as the Jewish Law condemned the Jews as sinners because we, like the ancient Israelites, fail to live up to it. If we have not internalised the concept of law, which is not dependent on the whims and fancies of the rich and the powerful, we will continue to fail our democracy and our Constitution.

If history is any guide, then one has to conclude that democracy will not succeed in India any more than it did in ancient Greece. How can the voice of corrupt people be the voice of God? Plato, the philosopher, studied Greek democracy and called it the worst kind of political system. In its place, he proposed that philosopher kings— like Brahmins—should rule.

The voice of ordinary people began to be respected as the voice of God in nations such as Great Britain and America, only because the people opened their hearts to God's Spirit for their inner spiritual transformation. They understood spirituality in the light of Psalm 1; as meditating on God's holy Law. By allowing God's word to renew their minds, poor people earned the right to hold their rulers and priests accountable in step with what is true and good.

It is right to celebrate our Constitution, but more than celebration is needed if our nation is to be transformed into a nation that reflects the ideals of our Constitution.

Chapter Twenty-six
Mathematics + Spirituality = Development

Why did the church's "Widows Fund " become an enormous commercial success? Widows and orphans were helpless; so, what prevented religious leaders, businessmen, politicians and bureaucrats from looting the fund in their custody? Why did our religious leaders ask our widows to commit sati instead of innovating comparable systems to take care of them?

In the holy city of Gangapur, two preachers were most renowned. Gyananand enthralled his audience by explaining that the Roman numerals (I, II, III, IV, V, etc.) could not have produced Western science, technology, banking, or economic development. They were inherently incapable of calculating mathematical units such as percentages or economic units such as compound interest. Dhyananand would then describe the accomplishments of Indian mathematicians such as Brahmagupta (seventh century), Mahavira (ninth century), and Bhaskara (twelfth century). The two never failed to mention that the world of modern finance owes its existence to the unknown sage who may have been a Brahmin and may have meditated on the banks of Mother Ganges, as he came up with the all-important mathematical concept of shoonya (zero).

Uma Devi was one of their favourite devotees. In fact, all the "holy" men were fond of her because whenever an ascetic went to her door, she always sent one of her children with freshly cooked food. She had made it a morning habit to set aside the first portion of the food for sadhus, who had renounced their own wives, children, and parents, in order to find enlightenment. Her piety, however, did not prevent the god Saturn from devouring her husband along with her youngest son. The truck that hit his scooter simply vanished. The tragedy became even more terrible because the scooter's insurance had run out. Her husband had chosen not to renew it, since he was thinking of getting a loan for a small car for the family. Uma's world fell apart; she was too shattered to be comforted even by these saints.

"Shall I commit sati?" she inquired of them in desperation.

"It is illegal," they counselled, "but dharma still accrues to a widow who chooses that sacred path."

"But what will happen to my children?" she cried.

"The scriptures say that your karma will benefit seven generations," they consoled her, looking at her daughter (nine) and son (seven).

The true story

Uma's tragic story is made up to help us understand the cultural factors that prevented Indian/ Arabic numerals from developing a socio-economic system to support widows and orphans. As Hindu apologists assert, our mathematical innovations became foundational tools for the amazing development of the West, as illustrated by the Widows Fund in Scotland. That fund began modern insurance and risk management that undergird contemporary economic life.

The Scottish Widows Fund was originally called a "Fund for a Provision for the Widows and Children of the Ministers of the Church of Scotland." It was the first modern, mathematics-based insurance company in the world. It provided an innovative "scientific" alternative to other ways of dealing with widows— asylums, lotteries, ponzi schemes, prostitution, starvation, or sati.

The fund, which grew to over £100 billion, has served as a midwife to tens of thousands of economic enterprises. It has also supported educational and philanthropic initiatives such as India's oldest continuously running liberal arts coolege, the Scottish Church College in Calcutta (1836), and the Scottish orphanage for girls in Mumbai that became Bombay Scottish School (1847). It began a scientific system of risk management that made it possible for people to borrow large amounts of capital to start new ventures across the continents and now even to get humans into outer space.

This widows fund was created by two Christian pastors in Scotland, Robert Wallace (1697-1771) and Alexander Webster (1708-1784). Both of them were mathematicians and Bible preachers. While we were condemning our upper caste widows in India to lifelong solitary confinement, if not to the flames of their husband's funeral pyres, the pro-life, pro-sex, pro-marriage, pro-widow spirituality of these pastors came together with the best-available mathematics to create the world of modern finance.

Unlike our saints who had to renounce their own wives and children, these Protestant pastors were both married because the Bible teaches that the physical world, including the human body and sexuality, are created by a good God who declares them "good." God does not want godly men to separate from the material world. He wanted Adam and Eve to become one in order to harness and channel their sexual energy to establish a family that will produce and nurture children to fill the earth and govern it by establishing human culture. This outlook or world-and-lifeview enabled Robert Wallace to write a pioneering study, "An Essay on the Principle of Population." He became the Moderator of the Church of Scotland; that is, the head of his denomination, like an Archbishop or a Shankaracharya.

Like Wallace, Webster also began his career as a minister (pastor) in the Church of Scotland, in Culross in Fife. There he met and married Mary Erskine of Alva. His love for his own wife as well as a deep concern for his friends' widows motivated him to team up with Wallace and use his training as a mathematician to solve widows' problems. In 1748, he published his *Calculations*, which set forth the scientific principles on which their scheme for widow pensions was based. The other mathematical prodigy who helped refine their innovation was Colin MacLaurin who had improved upon Newton's theories when he was only fourteen years old! MacLaurin was himself an orphan who grew up with his uncle—also a pastor. Unfortunately, MacLaurin died while he was still too young to see the Scottish Widows Fund flourish.

In their day, if a minister died, his widow and orphans received a stipend from the church for six months; after that, they were on their own. This was unacceptable to these two mathematician pastors because the Bible told them that "Religion that God our Father accepts as pure and faultless is this: to look after orphans and widows in their distress and to keep oneself from being polluted by the world" (James 1:27). Wallace gathered and tabulated the available information about pastors, widows, and orphans from all the churches in Scotland. Using the system of actuarial calculation and five other mathematical principles developed in Europe (not in India), the two of them estimated exactly how much premium each pastor would need to contribute to create a fund that would make it possible to (a) take care of the widows, as well as (b) to invest prudently to make the fund grow. Their calculations, predictions, and investment decisions turned out to be so exact that their system began to be followed by all the insurance companies that came after them. In 1754, Webster published *Zeal for the Civil and Religious Interests of Mankind Commended*. His work helps us understand how this milestone in the history of modern finance was a result of civil (scientific) interests, combined with religious (biblical) interests. Webster's work was of such high quality that in 1755, the government commissioned him to obtain data for the first census of Scotland.

Democratic spirituality

The Wallace-Webster financial innovation succeeded because of another cultural ingredient—the democratic structure of the Scottish church. The Greek philosopher Plato (429–347 BC) had condemned democracy as the worst of all political systems. That is why the spread of Greek culture, called Hellenization, did not stir a desire for democracy in the ancient world.

It was the Protestant Reformation's return to the Bible which birthed "modern" democracy in the Scottish church (and the Republican system of government in America). Reforming the church included replacing the autocratic rule of bishops and popes by the rule of democratically elected elders. The reformers followed the New Testament pattern of elders governing local churches. In appointing elders to manage church affairs and finances, Christ's apostles, in turn, followed an Old Testament pattern. After delivering the Hebrews from their slavery in Egypt, God instructed Moses to ask the twelve tribes to "Choose some wise, understanding, and respected men from your tribes, and I will set them over you..... So, I [Moses] took the leading men of your tribes, wise and respected men, and appointed them to have authority over you" (Deuteronomy 1:13– 15). The people chose their leaders and through Moses (and, after the coming of Jesus the Lord, through the apostles), but it was God who anointed them. Protestant nations were able to apply this "democratic" idea to nation states only because they had succeeded in reforming the church.

"The voice of the people" can be "the voice of God" only if the people grow in their knowledge of God and if their character becomes godly. If the people are corrupt, then their voice becomes the voice of the devil. This, as we shall see, is the problem now facing secularised democratic nations in the West. Far too many people in these nations no longer want to take the responsibility to work, earn, save, wisely invest, and take care of their neighbours, widows, orphans, refugees, and other victims of natural or man-made evils. They want their governments to tax or borrow from productive people and spend it on their welfare.

Why did the Church's "Widows Fund" become an enormous commercial success? Widows and orphans were helpless; so, what prevented religious leaders, businessmen, politicians, and bureaucrats from looting their funds in their custody? Why did our religious leaders ask our widows to commit sati instead of innovating comparable systems to take care of them?

Two factors were critical for the fund's success: a genuine, grass-roots democracy in the Scottish church and the godly character cultivated by a church centered, Bible-based Liberal Arts education. Ordinary church members elected wise and God-fearing elders and held them accountable; the elders elected presbyteries; which elected synods, the General Assembly, as well as the Moderator. On 12 May 1743, Wallace was elected the Moderator of the General Assembly of the Church of Scotland. The assembly approved his scheme. That enabled him to submit it to the Lord-Advocate in London, who framed it into a legislative measure and superintendent its safe progress into an Act.

The Widows Fund succeeded not simply because of mathematics but also because

All education, religious or secular, was Church's domain; the University of Edinburgh is still the institution that trains the pastors for the Scottish Church.

The biblical spirituality transmitted through the church, school, and university, nurtured honest, productive, compassionate, and public-spirited character.

The Bible's emphasis on human sinfulness required institutionalising accountability even among religious leaders, and

The biblically derived idea of local church-based grassroots democracy promoted responsible leadership all the way to the top.

Wallace was elected, not because he bribed, bullied, or manipulated voters, but because he came up with a scheme that made compelling sense. He followed the example of Joseph in the book of Genesis, who saved Egypt and its surrounding nations from a 7-year-long spell of drought and famine.

The foregoing may be hard to believe for fellow Indians because they know that many churches in India, established by Western denominations and handed over to Indian Christians, are now as corrupt as our public institutions. The financial corruption began as theological corruption as seminaries began to doubt God's revelation and trust the "fallen" human mind. Yet, sceptics may change their mind if they look at a typical Bible-based local church in India that is supported by donations from members or at a genuine all-India organisation such as the Union of Evangelical Students of India (UESI) that is built and run mainly by contributions from its members.

The so-called mainline churches that inherited prime properties and institutions tend to be corrupt because (a) their wealth does not come from their members, (b) they have undermined grass-roots democracy, and (c) they have replaced the Bible with human imagination.

A biblical church is fundamentally different from a typical Hindu temple. A devotee who goes to worship in a temple and donates money is not a "member" of that temple. He has no authority to scrutinise its accounts. In theory, the government can scrutinise a temple's account. In practice, however, our wealthy gurus and temples have learned the art of keeping politicians and civil servants in their pockets. In contrast to our Indian religious establishments, in the democratically organised churches, the donor is a member; he or she elects the elders and the treasurer; he or she approves or disapproves the budget and the accounts.

Of course, there were and are plenty of sinful Protestants; and corrupt people always seek to control public funds. The Presbyterian structure, however, was designed for sinful people. It sought to make them godly but also instituted wise structures to minimise the abuse of public funds. Transparency of institutions and rules that governed the church and the Widows Fund as well as public knowledge of the private lives of the church leaders helped generate the trust that ensured the fund's success.

It also helped that the original nine-hundred and thirty contributors to the fund were all pastors and that the fund was created to look after their wives and children. They were among the most learned and public-spirited members of the community. They understood the rules and helped refine and enforce them. The success of democratic institutions depends on the knowledge and character of their members. For example, many attempts to establish medical insurance companies in India have failed (in spite of our mathematical aptitude) because of the poor character of participating members, doctors, pharmacists, agents, and their lawyers. If insurance money is claimed for people who do not suffer from any disease, and for operations and medical procedures that have not been performed, then the calculations behind premiums become invalid.

Impact: Economic and political

The Widows Fund was a wonderful "welfare" scheme. It originated as a capitalistic or free-market enterprise. It operated under the law of the land, but was neither controlled by politicians nor run by bureaucrats. Why did deeply religious men multiply the fund's capital through wise business investments? Why didn't they take sannyas from moneymaking? They made money because they followed the Lord Jesus, who, in the spirit of the Old Testament, commended such economic stewardship—turning five bags of gold into ten—as true spirituality (Matthew 25:15– 17). People joined the fund because they trusted their community leaders with their money, and their trust was not betrayed. Today, however, because the fund is being run by completely secular people, it is not growing as it used to.

The fund's initial success in taking small amounts of money from lots of simple people and taking care of their families had a profound impact on global politics. It tempted politicians to imitate it and turn entire nations into welfare states. This political attempt began in Germany with Otto van Bismarck's social insurance legislation in 1880 and soon spread to Europe, the USSR, Japan, and the USA, both by the so-called "Right" and even more by the "Left", that is, by Socialist or Communist parties.

The idea was good: The state will take wealth from those who created it and use it to take care of everyone from cradle to the grave. Taking citizens' wealth was, of course, easy. Governments, however, are not structured to use other people's money to create wealth. Unscrupulous and arrogant rulers use public funds for their glory. They waste money even if they don't actually loot it. The worst part is that when a welfare state seems to succeed, it destroys citizens' the character. That, for example, is one of Japan's problems today. It took the concept of a welfare state farther than any European nation. But if the state is going to take care of you from birth to death, why would you take the trouble to bring up children and nurture your own family?

The Japanese did not lose interest in sex, yet Japan's population has been declining. That means that the number of citizens who will work and pay tax is diminishing. A population that does not reproduce itself is unsuitable for states' welfare schemes because they are unfortunately usually designed as Ponzi schemes. They depend on more and more people working, earning, and paying taxes to support retired people and those who no longer have the ability or willingness to hold down a job. So why are Japanese not having children? Japan did not have the Ten Commandments that included "You shall not covet your neighbour's wife" and "You shall not commit adultery." Japanese don't consider these as divinely given moral absolutes. Once Japan became a secular welfare state, people saw no need to take the trouble to harness sexual energy to build families that would produce and nurture children. A decline in population means a decline in taxpayers. Governments of Europe and America have followed the same folly. The welfare state has undermined the Ten Commandment that required children "To honour your father and mother." The Commandment presupposes that a man and a woman will undertake the tough responsibility to become a husband and a wife. That together they will produce children and assume the challenging responsibility to bring them up as good and productive citizens. Thanks to the welfare state and the availability of free sex, free contraceptives, and abortions, the West's own population is declining. People are choosing not to marry or not to have children. Mothers are aborting their babies, fathers, and increasingly mothers, are abandoning their spouses and children in favour of other partners. Taking care of the elderly became the responsibility not of the children but of the state. States are importing immigrants, hoping that they will bring up children who will pay for the elderly. This gigantic social experiment to live without God's law is backfiring now since the so-called welfare state has replaced the "Protestant work ethic." Valuing productive work or seeing work as sacred is what created the modern economic miracle. Secular "entitlement culture" makes people dependent on a "nanny state." This culture believes that citizens and even illegal aliens have the right to this, that, and the other, but no corresponding obligation to create wealth to look after themselves, their families, and their neighbours— especially widows, orphans, refugees, and other poor. That is why the West is becoming backward.

Meanwhile, we are "backward" in spite of our mathematical genius, because our culture has lacked a spirituality that promotes the creation of wealth, and a passion to use wealth to love our neighbours as ourselves. We have now learned Western mathematics and their application to economics, but in order to move forward, we also need to avoid the follies of Western secularism and discover the deliberately ignored and therefore now-unknown spiritual secrets of Western civilization.

Chapter Twenty-seven
William Carey:
The Wrecker of Vedic India?

"Even the Buddha was not able to damage Vedic culture as deeply as William Carey did."

William Carey was the nastiest[1] Englishman that ever came to India," said Mr. R. M. Pandit, my fellow-passenger. We were both going to England. His mission was to research Carey in connection with his 250th anniversary on 17 August 2011. Panditji's confident manner encouraged me to ask: "Who was Carey? How was he nasty to us?"

"In England, he was just a chamar, a cobbler. In 1793, he violated the British Parliament's ban on missionary activity in India and slipped in as an undercover Baptist missionary. He started the chain reaction that culminated in our day in a chamar woman becoming the ruler of UP—the very heartland of Hinduism."

"Why should that be so worrying?" I wondered out loud. "After all, Ms. Mayawati is dependent on Brahmins, and they can easily ditch her in the next election."

"I'm not concerned about one Mayawati," clarified Panditji. "My concern is that Carey brought to India certain cancer cells that have continued to multiply. They are infecting Hindu parties such as the BJP. Why do you think the BJP routinely appoints Shudras as chief ministers in the states it rules? Why can't it respect Hindu culture and promote professional rulers?" "I'm sorry, Panditji," I said sheepishly, "but I've no idea what you're talking about. If Carey was

---

[1] Rajiv Malhotra and Aravindan Neelakandan describe William Carey as one of the "nastiest Evangelists" in their book *Breaking India: Western Interventions in Dravidian and Dalit Faultlines* (Bhopal: Amaryllis, 2011), p. 338. R. M. Pandit mentioned in this article is a composite character, and the author's conversation with him is a literary device—not an actual incident.

born two hundred and fifty years ago, how is he responsible for what the BJP does today? If he was really the worst Englishman, why don't we hear more about him?"

Panditji seemed eager to educate me: "Other Europeans came to colonise and loot India militarily, politically, and economically, but William Carey came to change India. He pioneered the missionary movement with a goal to colonise our minds, harvest our souls, and destroy our culture. This is the worst kind of colonialism."[2]

"I'm afraid you have to explain to me how one colonises the mind," I requested the scholar.

"Why do you think that a Shudra in Tamil Nadu and a Dalit in Bihar both designate themselves as 'Dravidians'? Their forefathers saw themselves as an intrinsic part of the Aryan culture. Who changed our language of caste into that of distinct races—Aryans and Dravidians? Prior to Carey, some European scholars had taken an interest in Indian languages and literature. But he turned that academic curiosity into missionary mischief and inspired other missionary-linguists to build on these foundations."

"I've never heard this before," I assured Panditji.

My inquisitiveness encouraged him to explain: "Hindu sages engineered a harmonious society. Caste categorised us along a family's expertise. It allowed parents to teach their children how to excel in their family's profession. How can someone who milks cows teach his son to govern a state or navigate the sea? You tell me, do all human beings appear equal to you? Did the white Christians in America treat their black slaves as equal?"

"Definitely not," I said, "but Mahatma Phule was a contemporary of Abraham Lincoln, and he praised devout Christians for fighting against their fellow whites to emancipate black slaves. That is why the blacks in America love the Bible even more than the white people.

---

[2]This point is argued by Arun Shourie in his book *Harvesting Our Souls: Missionaries, Their Designs, Their Claims* (New Delhi: ASA Publications, 2000).

Didn't President Obama put his hand on Lincoln's Bible to take his oath of office?"

"The myth that God made all human beings—male and female—equally in his image does come from the Bible. But educated people believe in Evolution. Of course, no one has actually seen a fish evolve into a bird, but evolution confirms what our sages taught that some people are more evolved than others. How can everyone evolve equal? Evolution presupposes the fact of inequality, but a chamar, Carey, wanted us to believe the Bible's myth of human equality. He converted ignorant people and required them to break caste by eating together." "What strategies did he use to change India?"

"One was to propagate the myth that men and women were created equal; his mission started educating girls as well as boys."

"What's wrong with that?"

"You only change what you don't like. In order to change India, Carey had to misrepresent our culture."

"In what ways?"

"He published papers against the nobility of upper-caste women. who committed sati by climbing on to the funeral pyres of their deceased husbands to join them in the afterlife. His paper launched the campaign that got the British government to abolish the sacred tradition of sati."

"Really? I always heard that it was Raja Ram Mohan Roy who stopped widow-burning."

"Roy was Carey's disciple. A Sanskrit scholar, Hariharananda Vidyabagish, took Ram Mohan Roy to William Carey to learn English. The three of them fabricated the Maha Nirvana Tantra (The Book of the Great Liberation). It pretended to codify ancient Sanskrit law, proving that the Hindu scriptures did not require a widow to commit sati. For decades, the British courts yielded to the authority of this book in interpreting the Hindu law. Using that spurious book in law courts made Roy and the Tagore clan wealthy. Roy parted company with Carey and his mission because he became a Unitarian Christian. But throughout his life, he advanced Carey's agenda to change India. Along with the missionaries, he became the primary reason why Macaulay ruled that the Company's money should be used to teach English, not Sanskrit. They wanted to inject English ideas into Indian vernaculars. Roy followed Carey in condemning the very core of Hinduism— worship of idols and nature. He smuggled Christianity into Bengal, disguising it as Brahmo Samaj. His college was a platform for missionaries such as Alexander Duff."

Trying to make sense of what I was hearing, I asked: "What exactly did Carey do to corrupt India?"

"Speaking on a popular level, why is Hindi our 'national' language; why not Sanskrit?" Panditji fired back.

"You tell me," I said to him. "You seem to know."

"Sanskrit united India culturally. It preserved our harmony and genius. In order to translate the Bible into every Indian language, Carey mastered Sanskrit and prepared its dictionary. He wasn't serving Sanskrit. His objective was to make it easy for other Bible translators to understand the dialects inspired by Sanskrit and to turn them into literary languages via Bible translation. Do you know that the Bible is the most translated book in India? By developing Indian languages, missionaries divided us linguistically. If scriptures are available in your own mother tongue, why would you need a priest who has spent decades mastering Sanskrit? Once priests become irrelevant, so does our sacred culture."

"That sounds like unnecessary fear-mongering to me."

"It is necessary to be afraid. You can see the practical consequences of missionary strategy in Sri Lanka, Tamil Nadu, and also Andhra."

"What exactly are you referring to?"

"Who caused Sri Lanka's terrible civil war? It was European scholars who replaced the notion of caste by race and divided the people into Sinhalese Aryans and Tamil Dravidians. Tamil Nadu is next. I don't know Tamil, but it is an ancient language. But it does not predate Sanskrit. That mischievous idea is being promoted by missionaries."

"Is it true that missionary-linguists like Robert Caldwell and G. U.

Pope developed modern Tamil?"

"That is true. They followed Carey, but disagreed with him when they argued that Tamil grew independently of Sanskrit. Their strategy was to forge a Dravidian identity in opposition to Aryan. It implied that just as Sinhalese-speaking Aryans colonised Dravidians in Sri Lanka, Sanskrit-speaking Aryans had colonised them in India. Dravidians are revolting now because missionaries have taught them that the Brahmins had colonised Dravidian culture."

"Is this anything serious?"

"It is a tectonic fault line. In normal times, fault lines have no practical significance, but eventually they break apart whole continents. Bengali was the first language that Carey developed. His younger associates in Fort William College, such as Henry Martyn and Rev. Gilchrist, helped develop Urdu, Hindustani, and then Hindi. What came out of these literary developments? Carey's Bengali is now the national language of Bangladesh, and Sanskrit has disappeared from that part of India. Henry Martyn's Urdu rules Pakistan, and Sanskrit has gone from northwestern India. The Hindi that governs India is not the Hindi of Tulsidas. It is the Hindi of missionaries such as Gilchrist and Kellogg. That is Carey's ultimate legacy: Sanskrit that preserved our literature, scriptures, and culture seems destined for the dustbin of history. Even Hindu ashrams in the Himalayas now run English-medium schools, while they ought to be running Sanskrit universities."

"So did William Carey develop Indian vernaculars in order to divide and weaken us?"

"I am on my way to England to research his real motives. In public, of course, his followers argue that Europe was reformed when scholars like Wycliffe, Luther, and Tyndale began translating the Bible into the common man's languages, such as English and German. They say that you cannot have a government of the people unless it operates in the language of the people. In the sixteenth century, Paris University in France, Oxford and Cambridge in England, and Wittenberg in Germany, all taught in Latin. French, English, and German had no literature that any university could use.

The Bible translators changed that. They enriched vernaculars, making it possible for them to become the languages of learning. law and governance. That, in turn, made it possible for anyone to go to college and develop his potential. Carey claimed that he was bringing a similar reform to India. His work as a Hugust translator would open up the Indian mind. People would be able to read the scriptures and secular literature in their mother tongues and decide for themselves what is true. They wouldn't need the expertise of the priests."

"Are you suggesting that Carey developed Indian languages in order to democratise intellectual power? That he made knowledge available to everyone, including Shudras and women?"

"No! Along with his colleagues, he did start the first vernacular college in Serampore that used Bengali as a medium of instruction. It grew into India's first university, not owned by the British Raj, Carey himself taught astronomy, botany, and forestry—besides languages and, of course, the Bible. Carey's real motive was to educate us in order to convert us. His faith in the Bible made him such a bigot that he could not appreciate the devotion of the Hindus who sacrificed their children to the Mother goddess. He called it infanticide. That was his first attack on Hinduism,"

"What else did he do to weaken Brahminism?"

"In order to publish the Bible in Indian languages, attack Hinduism, and to pressurise the government to change our traditions, Carey brought the modern press to British India—both journalism as well as the printing press. At that time, we didn't make the kind of paper needed for the mechanical press, so his mission began manufacturing paper. To mechanise manufacturing, Carey installed a steam engine. That, in turn, started an industrial revolution, which weakened our cottage industry."

"But did his writing and publishing actually damage India?" "Have you ever wondered why, after six decades of Independence, India is still governed by a penal code written by Lord Macaulay? Isn't that enough to show the effectiveness of intellectual colonisation? Macaulay was simply following William Carey, who wrote in 1792, that is, one year before he came to India, that the spread of the Gospel of Jesus Christ would transform India. It will replace the rule of wise men with the kingdom of God, that is, theocratic laws derived from the Bible."

"Panditji, you have said so many new things that my head is spinning. Can you summarise what you are telling me about William Carey?"

"I haven't described a fraction of the mischief that William Carey began in the four decades that he spent here. It was not colonialism but Christianity that turned India upside down. If there was no Carey, there would be no missionaries, no Raja Ram Mohan Roy, no Tagores, no Keshab Chandra Sen, no Jotiba Phule, no Ambedkar, Periyar, or Kanshi Ram. Sanskrit and our sages would have kept India united in one culture. That unity would be much deeper than the political-legalconstitutional unity that the British gave us in line with their biblical idea of a nation state."

"Vedic India," I said to Mr. Pandit, "may have been better than modern India. But from all that you are telling me, it seems that for better or for worse, William Carey, not Mahatma Gandhi, is the Father of the modern Indian nation. Without him, we might have a cultural India but no political India,"

"That is true. Even the Buddha was not able to damage Vedic culture as deeply as William Carey did. The Buddha did reject caste, but he was wise enough to accept karma-reincarnation as an explanation of self-evident inequality. The Buddha agreed that we are born unequal because of our karma. But William Carey came to transform India. The movement that he began has become incredibly potent. Today there are at least 80,000 full-time Indian missionaries. They are transforming grassroots communities where no church exists. Like Carey, many of them serve the poorest of the poor, the lowest of the low. They educate and uplift the downtrodden, firing their hearts with dreams and ambitions that could be exploited by all kinds of disruptive movements. Don't you see, Carey laid the foundations for breaking India!"

"Panditji," I said hesitatingly, "you are a scholar. I am a simple person. But somehow, I feel that many Indians would think that the seed Carey planted was for breaking the prison that kept our people backward. To be honest, even I can't comprehend why you would refer to the Father of Modern India as 'the nastiest Englishman."

"Don't worry," Panditji replied with an air of superiority, "even our convent-educated intellectuals don't understand our history and the damage done by missionaries' conspiracy. But I can explain my point with a simple analogy..." (*Continued in Conclusion*)

Chapter Twenty-eight
Conclusion: A Conspiracy of Hope[*]

Panditji's patience was exemplary, as he explained to me why William Carey was "the nastiest Englishman" that came to India.

Think of Hinduism, said Mr. R. M. Pandit, as a mighty citadel made of solid stones. That enabled Vedic culture to withstand a thousand years of external aggressions. William Carey and the missionaries who followed him became the worst invaders because they did not attack us with guns. They took Jesus' strategy of the seed and a sower seriously.

Can you explain it to me, please? I requested.

Carey was like a little parrot that brought the fruit of a banyan tree and perched on the walls of our citadel. Other parrots followed him. They dropped some seeds on the wall. Most were eaten up by insects and birds. A few germinated but died without soil or moisture. Just a few seeds fell in cracks where enough dirt had accumulated. The sun's rays did not penetrate deep enough to dry up the moisture. Those dark and inaccessible spots allowed the seeds to take roots.

One day a plant appeared, growing out of the wall. It looked too tiny to be taken seriously. The caretakers assumed that the plant would die out during the summer. It did seem to wither but it reappeared during the monsoon. It caused no worries because it was not bigger than before. Its shiny leaves looked pleasant on those barren rocks. We tolerated it because we like greenery.

No one saw the real growth that was taking place in hidden places. The roots were wrapping themselves around one rock after another.

Some of the roots eventually struck water and nourishment. Then the plant began to thicken and broaden the cracks. By the time the caretakers decided to pull out the plant, it was too late. It couldn't be

---

[*]This Conclusion continues the conversation with Mr. R. M. Pandit begun in the previous chapter.

uprooted without knocking down the wall. But if they didn't deal with the tree, it would breach the entire citadel.

The missionaries who brought the Bible to India knew that they were bringing a seed that had torn apart the Holy Roman Empire. It had transformed Europe, and they were confident that it would demolish the citadel that had kept our culture intact.

But aren't our temples flourishing? Haven't our gurus become superstar celebrities?

Our gurus and godmen have indeed become wealthy. They can fly around in private jets. Perhaps that is what prevents them from seeing that the walls of their citadel are being breached. The backwards are walking out of the citadel, believing that their home has been their prison. There is a huge demographic shift, but no one seems to be noticing it.

Does the last census show any cause for concern?

That is my point: the census counts the leaves that are visible. It cannot track invisible roots.

What are you seeing that makes you so militant?

My researchers have just uncovered a conspiracy that will make India unrecognisable within a generation or two.

What's that?

Some Indian missionaries are preparing to turn every local church, in every village and town, into a university classroom. *That is impossible!*

Not really.

Their plan is to follow the Wikipedia model to create a curriculum online. They call it a BA in Nation-building. This high-quality curriculum, created by hundreds of experts from around the world, will be made available online to everyone for free. Every university will be induced to use it. The classes will be held in churches. Every church will be equipped with an Academic Pastor who will invite ten to fifteen students to come to the local church, Monday to Friday, for four years to earn a BA. The lessons and professors will be online, in DVDs, and in books. Students will be able to use their phones, iPads, and tablets, to take lessons and talk to teachers and experts.

But how can churches offer vocational training?

The Academic Pastor will place students as interns in local businesses, professionals, and NGOs."

But what about science practicals that require laboratories? They plan to contract existing labs in schools and colleges and encourage industries to build labs for local students,

But surely not all subjects can be taught online?

Their plan is to encourage students to go to a college for short intensive courses when necessary to study what cannot be taught locally,

So, why is this so dangerous?

This plan will give enormous manpower to every church. The course will require every student to spend at least two evenings a week serving others. The church will use this massive manpower to serve every slum, every village, and every locality.

So, why should that be a concern?

Can't you see that every illiterate mother will go to the church in her neighbourhood asking for volunteers to help her children with their homework; every widow will go to the local pastor asking him to send two or three volunteers to fix her roof. A church may be meeting in a mud hall with a thatched roof, but it will become the centre of university-level education and service that fights hunger, poverty, and disease. Their aim is to transform whole communities.

This sounds like a revolution! No wonder you are worried. Actually, I can't say that I am worried. There are significant currents developing within the church that could sabotage these conspiracies.

Such as?

Missionaries such as William Carey established universities, but now most American missions have little interest in higher education. In fact, some have turned against basic literacy. They dislike terms such as illiterate. They "honour" illiterate people as "oral learners," and prefer to give them stories, not university degrees.

What brought about this change in missionary strategy?

Some of their theologians started teaching that their old strategies of transforming oral dialects into literary languages, translating the Bible into languages that no one reads, and then teaching people to read their own language, delay the coming of the kingdom of God. Americans want to speed up God's timetable. They believe that as soon as they finish telling Bible stories to those tribes and castes that have not heard about Jesus Christ, the end of this Kaliyug will come, and Jesus himself will return to establish his rule for a thousand years. Wonderful fairytale ending!

You seem to be happy about this new strategy of Western missions.

Even illiterate parents know what is good for their children. They want their children educated. The new missionary strategy gives Hindu missions the chance of taking over the task of educating illiterate people.

And there is something else that helps me sleep a little better these days.

What is that?

Fortunately, many Americans now present Christianity as a story. And anyone can see that our stories are so much better than Bible stories. It has a few short parables, but it was never written as a story. Most of it claims to be real history. That is why James Cameron based *Avatar* on the story of Ram, not Jesus.

Earlier missions damaged us, because they presented Jesus as the Truth. They branded themselves not as storytellers but as "witnesses." That meant they were bearing witness to the truth while Hindu preachers were storytellers, peddling myths. Defining the conflict as Truth versus Myth was the single most important factor that enabled Christianity to destroy Greco-Roman mythology. Because of its passion for Truth, Christianity came with universities and claimed that it explores history and geology, physics and chemistry, biology, and archaeology because it is committed to pursuing truth. It was impossible for our myths to withstand such a commitment to truth. Fortunately, their new strategy is a game changer in our favour. A conflict between stories—ours and theirs—

is perfectly suited for us.

So, do you mean that, after all, you have no reason to fear?

No! NO! We have an immense challenge before us: These new missionaries who are planning to turn every thatched-roof church into a university centre are using the latest technology, but their worldview is old fashioned. They are as interested in truth as in service. American missions may want to protect our culture, including our illiteracy, but it is indigenous missionaries who have become dangerous. They are unabashedly committed to transforming our culture.

Can you imagine the consequences of every Shudra getting a world-class education in his own village?

We have nothing to fear from American missionaries who teach that upper caste followers of Jesus should not worship with lower-caste believers. This racism of Christian Americans fits well with our traditional culture. The problem is with these new Indian missionaries. They are taking the education revolution championed by reformers such as William Carey, Ram Mohan Roy, Alexander Duff, Jotirao Phule, and Bhimrao Ambedkar to its logical end. They are dangerous because they also carry their coffins on their heads. Jesus turned the world upside down because he called his disciples to take up their cross as they go out to make disciples/learners of every person, every tribe, every language group, and every nation.

Panditji, I would love to learn more from you, but you have given me so much information that I now need some time to close my eyes and think about what such an education revolution would do to the Backwards. So, please let me take my leave, namaste.

"This book establishes that Dalit-Bahujan backwardness is rooted in Hindu caste backwardness. The West's advancement, including science and technology, capitalism, and democracy, came out of the Bible's worldview and ethic. The earliest Indian to understand this was Mahatma Jotirao Phule. But his agenda was never carried to the logical end."

— Professor Kancha Ilaiah,
author of *Why I Am Not a Hindu*

"Humility is the first step in knowing the truth. To gain true freedom, a people must own their roots to bear fruit'. Vishal Mangalwadi exemplifies the meaning of this dictum. Sant Kabir says, 'Uncha paani na tike niche hi thaharaye, Nicha hoi so bhar piye, uncha pyasa jaye!" (The haughty will remain thirsty, but the lowly will be filled.). This book is an invitation to seek the Truth, even if it turns our world upside down.

— Sunil Sardar,
Executive Director,
Truthseekers International
(Satya Shodhak Samaj)

The Enlightenment myth has decisively collapsed. Scholars across the globe, and across ideological divides, agree that that social engineering has failed to deliver justice, equality, liberty and fraternity. In chapter after chapter, Vishal Mangalwadi demonstrates that only a genuine spiritual force can shatter the cultural constructs enslaving a large mass of humanity in South Asia, and especially in India.

— Professor Ashish Alexander,
Dean, School of Humanities and Social Sciences,
SHUATS, Prayagraj, India